WELCOME
to
Dennison Manufacturing Co.
ESTABLISHED 1844.   INCORPORATED 1878.

Its History, Products, Programs, and People

BY PATRICIA LAVIN
AND LAURA STAGLIOLA

FRAMINGHAM
HISTORY CENTER

Welcome to Dennison Manufacturing Co. is copyright 2015 by Patricia Lavin
ISBN: 978-0-692-51280-7

Published 2015 by the Framingham History Center
Framingham, Massachusetts
www.framinghamhistory.org

Table of Contents

Introduction

At the end of the day on Friday, August 15, 2013, the key turned for the last time. After 115 years in Framingham, the Dennison Manufacturing Company closed its doors here forever.

A year before the closure, the Framingham History Center (FHC) was invited to peruse the Dennison Archives. This historical collection had been recently returned to Framingham from California by the Avery Dennison Corporation. The archives, originally stored in Framingham, were sent to California when the Avery International Corporation of Pasadena and the Dennison Manufacturing Company merged in 1990.

The FHC was to select documents, catalogues, product samples, and other items of interest that would tell the Dennison story, and preserve its history now, and for future generations. It was also important to find good homes for archival items that the FHC would not be able to add to its collection.

The newly arrived archives, stored at Dennison's Bishop Street warehouse, consisted of one hundred plus boxes of assorted materials and twenty-two four drawer file cabinets. The collection included thousands of folders meticulously labeled and dated in chronological order from the mid-1800s to the late 1900s. There were also miscellaneous, and sometimes mysterious and puzzling items, quietly calling out for our attention.

What a sight as the key was turned, and the warehouse door opened to us for the first time in July of 2012! Sets of eyes merrily danced around the room wondering: where does one begin? Like children in a candy shop, we initially engaged in acts of excited exploration as we carefully surveyed all that appeared before us. Which drawer, which box shall we choose first? Under the tutelage and expertise of Dana Ricciardi, FHC curator, our efforts became discerning, organized and purposeful in the days and weeks that followed. Despite

Fred Bastien was employed by Dennison Manufacturing Co./ Avery Dennison Corp. for 33 years. Members of the Framingham History Center met Fred in 2012. He was in charge of maintenance for the Bishop Street building where the Dennison Archives were stored. Fred's work history, company stories and answers to questions added vitality to our archival discoveries. His affection for Dennison is summed up in these words: *"It was a good place to work. They were good to me."* **Fred turned the key that closed the last Dennison building on August 15, 2013.**

Box contains a glass slide of the Dennison Buildings in Framingham.

our initial feelings of being overwhelmed, the Dennison narrative began to gradually unfold before us. We were drawn in, and fascinated by the development, evolution and the many unique characteristics of this extraordinary American company. The Dennison story became our story, a blended narrative, to be shared in this chronicle of words and pictures gleaned from the boxes, files and miscellany of this remarkable collection.

Photo credit: Members of the Framingham History Center

Laura Stagliola.

Kevin Swope.

Pat Lavin (left) and
Susan Silva (right).

Nancy Prince (left) and
Dawne Buckley (right).

Nancy Prince and James King.

Susan Silva.

Paula Boulette &
Dana Dauterman Ricciardi (standing).

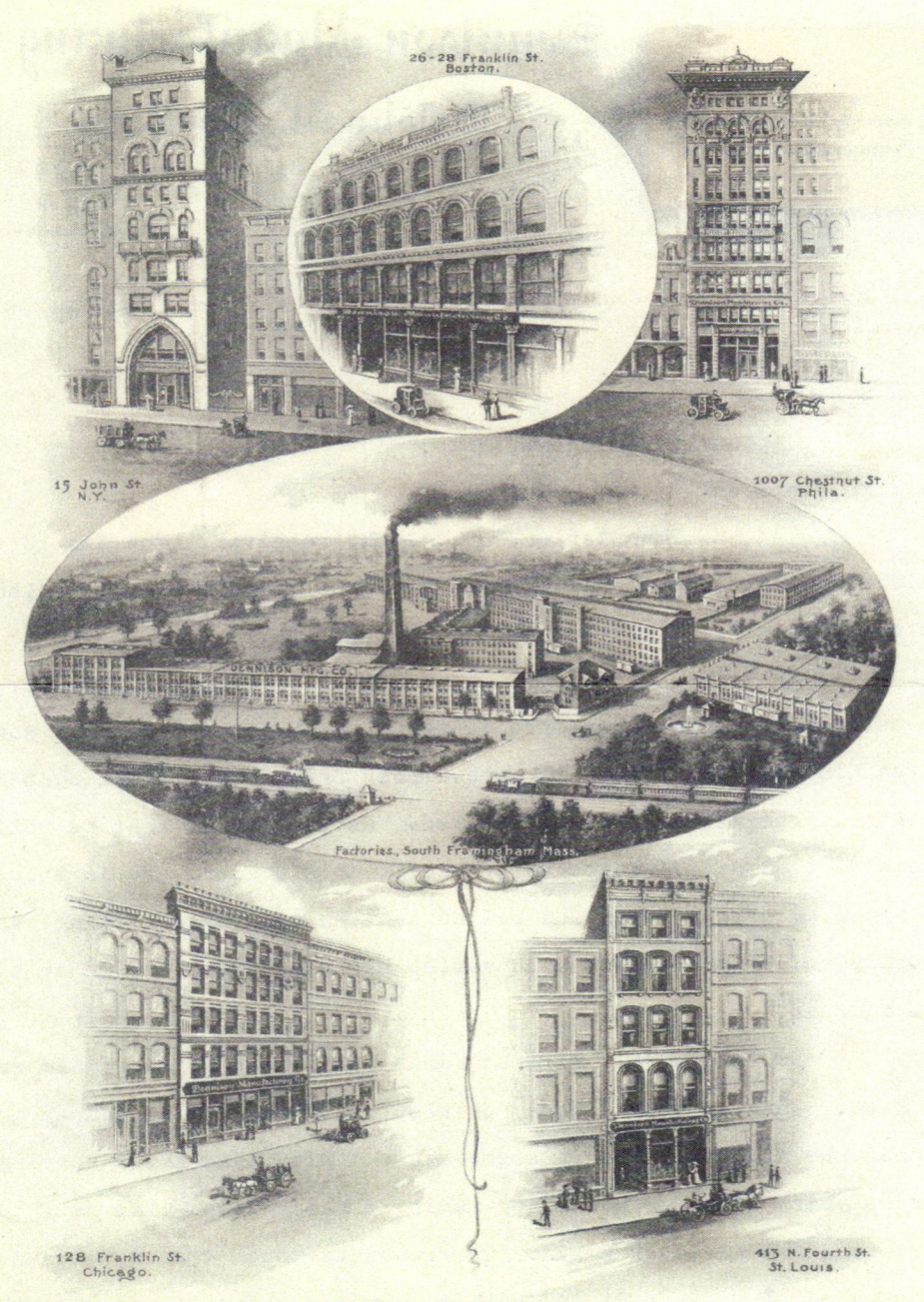

26-28 Franklin St.
Boston.

15 John St.
N.Y.

1007 Chestnut St.
Phila.

Factories., South Framingham Mass.

128 Franklin St.
Chicago.

413 N. Fourth St.
St. Louis.

Stores and Factories
of
Dennison Manufacturing Co.

Acknowledgments

Thank You To:

Avery Dennison Corporation for the gift of the Dennison Manufacturing Company Archives to the Framingham History Center. The desire to share this incredible history was the inspiration for *Welcome to Dennison Manufacturing Co.;*

Fred Bastien for suggesting a book about the Company in 2013, and for sharing his many stories and experiences as a Dennison employee;

Framingham History Center Director, Annie Murphy, for support, encouragement and manuscript suggestions;

Framingham History Center Curator, Dana Dauterman Ricciardi, Nancy Prince and James King for assistance in locating documents, images and historic information;

Town Historian, Fred Wallace for proofreading comments and research assistance;

Researcher, Ruthann Tomassini for expertise in tracking down those hard to answer questions;

Librarian, Martha Davidson for guidance in navigating the History Center's library collection.

Special Thanks To:

Susan Silva for research assistance, proofreading and especially for the many stimulating conversations as the book developed and grew;

Ruth Schwendeman for many hours of proofreading, editing and thoughtful suggestions that helped to clarify the text;

Graphic Designer, Nancy Stoodt for creating the beautiful layout of our book.

Opposite page: Back of letterhead, 1905.

The Dennison Story: *Product Evolution*

Aaron Dennison.

Colonel Andrew Dennison.

BOXES AND JEWELRY CARDS

The unexpected birth in 1844 of the box business at the Dennison homestead in Brunswick, Maine, marks the beginning of the Dennison Manufacturing Company story. In the mid-1800s, the jewelry trade in Boston had difficulty obtaining suitable boxes to showcase its merchandise. Merchants depended on a foreign import that was poorly constructed, not readily available, and often damaged upon arrival.

Aaron Dennison, a Boston watchmaker and jeweler, decided that he could make a better jewelry box than the clumsy, expensive European import. He had often devised the pieces necessary to repair watches and jewelry. Why not lessen the dependence on foreign supplies and give box making a try?

With a plan in mind, a $7.50 supply of pasteboard, and enameled and glazed paper in hand, Aaron headed to the family home in Brunswick, Maine where his father, shoemaker Colonel Andrew Dennison lived. He felt that his father's ability to cut and shape leather would help him craft a quality paper jewelry box.[1]

After close examination of sample paper boxes, Andrew sat down at his cobbler's bench. Glancing at his tools, he aptly picked up the old shoe knife and his trusty straight edge. Using these simple tools, he skillfully cut the pasteboard into paper box forms. When the forms were finished, Aaron's sisters, Julia and Matilda carefully put the boxes together and covered them with the fancy paper.

Pleased with the attractive finished product, Aaron took the boxes back to Boston where he sold them to local shopkeepers and prestigious jewelry houses. Among his first buyers was a firm, which would later be known as the Shreve, Crump & Low Company. These neatly constructed containers sold out immediately, and

Cobbler's bench.

demand surged. The superiority of the Dennison box was clearly recognized — excellent quality and elegant style.

To fill the need for ever-growing orders and speed up production, father and son worked diligently together, and successfully devised a box cutting machine. A patent for the machine was applied for and quickly granted. This ingenious mechanical invention was flawless in construction and produced the desired results. From handmade to machine made, the first American box company was born — Dennison & Company!

In 1844, ten workers were hired and new machinery was added to meet the rising demand. Three thousand dollars' worth of merchandise was sold in the Company's first year. As well as local merchants, wholesale jewelers from New York and many other cities placed orders for the new domestic boxes. Business was on the rise and the future appeared to be quite promising.

The second year brought an increase in sales and the beginning of steady growth and stability. Because of its initial and continued success, Aaron was now confident that the business was on firm footing and no longer demanded his full attention. While the selling of boxes and jewelry had been somewhat profitable, Aaron's true interest lay in watch-making. It was the crafting and production of an efficient quality timepiece, which kindled his passion. With this in mind, Aaron placed the operation of the Brunswick business into Colonel Dennison's capable hands.

Colonel Andrew and his daughter Julia admire the first jewelry box.

Aaron's early experiences repairing watches had taught him that a quality timepiece would only become a reality if watch production were based on the principle of interchangeable parts. He was inspired by the gun manufacturing techniques that he had observed at the Springfield Armory where interchangeable parts were manufactured. He knew uniformity of parts meant machine made. After much thought, Aaron's mechanical ingenuity, experimentation and perseverance bore fruit, and finally brought the longed for success as his machine became a reality. At his newly built Roxbury factory in 1851, his hand set the first machine into motion. From that moment on, watch-making was changed forever. Aaron's early inspiration led to the future foundation of the Waltham Watch Company. He has been honored with the well-deserved title, "Father of American Watch-making."

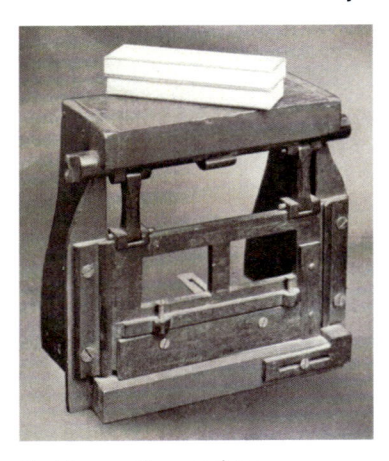

First box cutting machine.

Dennison homestead in Brunswick, Maine.

For his part, he would sell boxes from his Boston location, and continue to purchase and ship the supplies needed for box manufacturing in Brunswick.

Aaron then returned to his shop in Boston. He resumed the sale of jewelry and boxes, still yearning to be able to devote his full attention to the production of watches. In the latter part of the 1840s, two events occurred that enabled Aaron's dream to come true. In 1849, he acquired a partner, clockmaker Edward Howard, who agreed to join him in the manufacture of pocket watches using interchangeable parts. In the same year, Aaron sold his jewelry business. Shortly thereafter, he received the financial backing he needed from Samuel Curtis, a Boston manufacturer of mirrors.[2] At last watch-making could become his full time occupation.

Although Aaron was now retired from the box business, he knew that his father still needed an agent — a factory to sales go between. His younger brother, Eliphalet Whorf Dennison, (E.W.) had been working at the Boston jewelry shop as a salesman for a year before the business was sold. Aaron saw that E.W.'s genial manner and honest ways were attractive and easily drew in potential customers. Aware of these qualities, Aaron turned the responsibility of box sales and supplies over to his brother on October 1, 1849. E.W. took on this new opportunity with enthusiasm, envisioning endless possibilities for expansion and success if he managed his new position prudently.

Dennison's American made boxes grew in popularity. During the first year, E.W. and his father made a verbal agreement for profit sharing. Although profit was still quite limited, the business at the Brunswick homestead continued to hold its own. The family was working steadily and lived quite comfortably.

E. W. IN 1854

Eliphalet Whorf Dennison.

As a salesman, E.W. traveled to many cities and towns promoting his jewelry boxes. On these trips, he was always on the lookout for new ideas and products that would fill the needs and wants of the merchants with whom he did business. Soon, items such as jewelry cards, cotton and twine were added to broaden the popular Jewelers' Line. E.W. was also forever vigilant in searching for items to offer beyond the Jewelers' Line. He introduced special kinds of boxes to meet customer demands. Boxes for combs, wedding cakes, needles, flowers and hairpins were just a few of the new additions, which were met with enthusiasm.

It was in the 1850s that real change began to emerge. E.W. decided to further his product offerings and seek other business opportunities. He was ready to branch out! This brought him to his first salesroom and office at 203 Washington Street, Boston, in 1850.[3]

When it came to marketing, E.W. was definitely a man of detail. As he sold jewelry boxes to shop owners, he took notice of the small hand cut cards upon which the jewelry was placed for display. These homemade cards, haphazard and irregular in appearance, diverted the eye away from the jewelry's presentation. This small, but important item, would better serve the jeweler if it were consistent and uniform in size — it must be machine made. A perfectly cut card beckoned to E.W.'s ingenuity! Before long, meticulously finished jewelry cards, produced on his new invention, were presented for the first time to Boston dealers in 1851. Cards were followed by Dennison's own jewelers' cotton in 1854, which had previously been imported from Europe. So clever was E.W. in providing new items for his customers, that their wants soon became their needs, eventually making Dennison products a business essential!

The ongoing demand for a large quantity and reliable source of cardboard for boxes and now for jewelry cards, led E.W. to the cardboard and Bristol-board factory of Mr. Lamson Perkins in Roxbury, Massachusetts. At the Perkins' plant, he found the high quality stock that he needed and an exceptional manufacturing facility. After a congenial meeting, the two men made an agreement to become business associates; a relationship that would last for more than a quarter of a century. This move would prove to be a mutually profitable enterprise for both companies.

Wedding cake box, 1909.

Perkins factory.

OLD BRUNSWICK BOX FACTORY.

Dunlap Block on Maine Street
in Brunswick.

By 1850, E.W. had already been making monthly sales trips to New York City. What he soon discovered there, was not just new customers, but an extremely promising market. As a result, in 1855, he opened a small office in the jewelry district at 17 Maiden Lane to accommodate sales.[4] In order to manage the office full time, he hired Henry Hawks as his New York agent. One of E.W.'s customers, Mr. Fellows, a well-known jewelry wholesaler, had recommended Mr. Hawks for his "promptness, ability, and general intelligence." Mr. Hawks proved an excellent choice. His ability to run the office efficiently, eventually led to a partnership in 1863.

For the next few years, E.W. and his father manufactured boxes in Maine and sold them in Boston. However, coordinating the two locations often hampered the smooth flow of business. E.W. suggested they move the box making to Roxbury, closer to the market, but his father did not want to leave his Brunswick home. These challenges, along with probable competition and the tension of divided authority, prompted E.W. to buy his father's share of the business in 1855. He now hoped that production and marketing — factory and sales — would begin to merge and come together in a centralized location under his sole control. From this moment in time until his death in 1886, E.W. was Dennison's *leader and builder.*[5]

Boxes continued to be made at the Dennison homestead at 8 Everett Street in Brunswick, until the steady increase in business led to the need for more space. Although some boxes were briefly made in Newtonville, Brunswick became the manufacturing center by the 1860s. At first, the operation of the factory took place on more than one site until the entire business was moved to the Dunlap Block on Maine Street in Brunswick.[6] In the early 1880s, the Brunswick plant was operating at maximum efficiency, straining to keep up with incoming orders. Although 500 people were employed by 1890, more local workers were needed to keep pace with the demand for Dennison products. Gradually, over the next four years due to the labor shortage in Brunswick, the entire box department moved to the spacious Perkins' plant in Roxbury.

E.W. always kept the development and continuity of the business in mind. In the early 1870s, he began to think seriously about safeguarding Dennison & Company for the future and assuring its smooth passage on to the next generation. E.W.'s solution to his concern was incorporation.[7] It seemed logical to him that this should combine Perkins' exceptional manufacturing facility with Dennison's first-rate method of distributing goods to create a truly outstanding organization.

Although he tried many times to convince Mr. Perkins to join forces, Perkins was not interested in this joint venture. E.W. finally found the financial backing that he needed. Then, without further delay, he went ahead and incorporated on April 6, 1878 as Dennison Manufacturing Company for $150,000. E.W. became the Company president and Albert Metcalf was made treasurer. The following year, after many offers, Mr. Perkins agreed to sell his factory to E.W. for $85,000. E.W. now felt he owned the best card stock factory in the world. With the purchase of the Perkins' plant, tag production and profit soared. E.W.'s early desire to centralize was moving in the right direction.

Over the decades, the Jewelers' Line strove toward offering a wide variety of products.[8] From early common paper boxes came fine boxes, candy boxes, pen and pencil boxes, domed top boxes, satin covered boxes, boxes in nests, silverware boxes, celluloid boxes, telescope boxes, jewelry display fixtures, cases — and an overflowing raft of supplemental and specialty jewelry items!

Variety of display cases and boxes.

SHIPPING AND MERCHANDISE TAGS

It was in Boston that Dennison's most important product was developed, which would play a major role in the striking growth of Dennison & Company. The success of the jewelry card naturally paved the way for the Company's new enterprise: The Tag.

E.W.'s attention had often been drawn to the small tags attached to jewelry in shop owners' windows. He noticed the accompanying marking tags, like the jewelry cards, were hand cut by shop boys and clerks out of leftover paper and pasteboard. No two tags were alike. The untidiness and inconsistency of the tags marred the lovely appearance of the jeweler's display. In an attempt to offer shopkeepers a uniform product, E.W. imported jewelry tags from Europe in 1854. Unfortunately, the tags like the boxes were of inferior quality, making them very unappealing to the American market.

The positive response to the jewelry cards gave E.W. confidence that shopkeepers would buy a better line of quality, uniformly cut tags that appealed to the eye. After much thought and planning, he meticulously rearranged the dies in his jewelry card machine and put his newest merchandising idea into motion. The carefully altered machine worked by treadle, producing one tag at a time. At the front of the machine, the tags were collected by hand and put into bundles of one hundred. Later, each tag was strung with silk thread. The perfectly finished product was worthy of the finest jewelry!

First tag machine.

E.W. found a very enthusiastic market for his tiny jewelers' tags. Their uniform size and attractive appearance made the merchandise to which they were attached so pleasing to the buyer's eye. This wise decision quickly became "a source of continual profit."[9]

The popularity of the small jewelry tags, suggested that a large marking tag might be of benefit to merchants in other retail areas. When they were finally manufactured and became available, however, E.W. found there was very little interest in this new product. Thrifty shopkeepers claimed it was too extravagant to buy tags when they could use those cut by shop clerks from left over cardboard. Some convincing was needed! In order to make tradesmen more aware of the tag's advantages, E.W. visited furniture stores, clothing and other retail stores, pointing out the benefits of these large uniformly-made marking tags. At the same time, thousands of the large tags were freely given to potential customers. Woolen mills and dry goods companies were the first to be drawn to the tidy new marking tags, which finally turned the heads of other wholesale and retail dealers. It was quickly apparent to merchants that this was a simple means of boosting product sales.

The early tags were used primarily to state the product's price, size or number. E.W. soon noticed that many of the merchants had no fixed

Early merchandise broadside, 1859.

14

method of marking their goods with specific sales information. It was a rather hit or miss approach. After studying a product's features, E.W. devised a tag with standard information that fit the company's particular needs. As a result, specialized tags in a variety of sizes and shapes that contained just the right information began to take hold. By 1858, the sale of merchandise tags caught on and became exceptionally profitable. Quality, value, and personalization made Dennison & Company and "merchandise tag" synonymous. Once again E.W.'s foresight provided what merchants needed.

Further expansion of Dennison & Company occurred when Albert Metcalf was employed by E.W. in 1862. These two men first met at 203 Washington Street, Boston in 1850, where Mr. Harvey Richards, an Attleboro manufacturer of jewelry and E.W. shared a rented second floor salesroom. Albert was in charge of Mr. Richards' office and jewelry display, which was located in the front of the salesroom. The small rear section of this salesroom was occupied by E.W. It was in this rear space that he kept a small stock of boxes and produced his machine cut jewelry cards and tags.

E.W. and Albert began as acquaintances and soon became close friends. Albert took an interest in the Dennison product line and business. If E.W. were out, Albert would take charge of his merchandise — sell a box and some tags, charge them to what E.W. called the "scratch book," and make out a bill of sale. He willingly promoted the benefits of Dennison jewelry boxes, cards and tags to potential customers.

In 1856, Albert left Mr. Richards' jewelry business and tried other ventures with little success. During this time, E.W. tried several times to draw him into employment. At last in the summer of 1862, with some coaxing from E.W., Albert finally agreed to become a Dennison employee. He began as the general clerk and office manager. Albert clearly understood business and E.W. was certainly innovative and daring! Albert's astute attention to business organization and financial detail, and E.W.'s enthusiasm for new opportunity, combined to form a perfect balance. This winning combination led to a partnership in 1863.[10]

Looming on the horizon, the Dennison's newest invention was to be its *crowning glory — its road to fortune.* It would give this struggling business permanence, profitability, and a means to increase expansion at an extraordinary pace.

Shipping tags or "direction labels" had been in use for a long time. Linen tags with folded ends were imported from England, but handmade cardboard shipping tags were more often used by American merchants. With the approach of the Civil War, shipping tags took on an added importance. The imported linen tags became too expensive. Cheaper American tags with metal eyelets easily pulled away from the string and

Albert Metcalf.

packages were lost. Now, given transportation's overwhelming demand, E.W. saw an enormous opportunity and embraced this new challenge. He saw the need to quickly develop a satisfactory American shipping tag — a tag that would get merchandise safely to its destination. E.W. presented the problem of strengthening the paper tag

to his workers. William Stratton, his merchandising tag designer, devised a gummed washer to reinforce the hole. A paper washer on each side of the hole was a simple solution, a strong means of attachment. Stratton's ingenious invention was granted a patent in 1863.

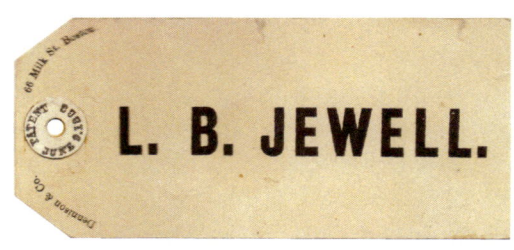

Shipping tag, 1865.

At this time E.W. was already buying a large supply of cardboard from the Perkins factory. Now with this new product to manufacture, he required a much larger working area. This prompted him to make arrangements to rent space at the Perkins plant where he would place his first shipping tag machine. In 1863, the rather awkward machine put out about 15,000 tags a day and delivered ten million tags to the marketplace in the first year. This might sound like a very impressive

number. However, Dennison found that the machine was expensive to run and felt that the ten million mark did not meet the immediate success that had been expected.

But, something quite remarkable did occur! As the shipping tag traveled, it carried an unexpected bonus. Printed on the circular reinforced patch, was the name Dennison & Company, which became an advertising tool as packages were shipped throughout the business world. This wonderful advertising surprise brought the recognition that the tag and the Company needed. At last there was a shipping tag that would stay — not stray. And buyers took notice of the Dennison name!

Two years later, with the need for tags increasing, a more efficient and productive machine was designed and built by E.W., Charles Sawyer, the Superintendent of the Perkins factory and Charles Moore. By 1872, four or five of these machines working at the same time could make as many as 300,000 tags in one day. The machine not only reduced cost, but led to the production of a stronger, more durable product.

At this time, Dennison was confronted with competition. Tags were now manufactured by companies in the United States and Europe. To combat this

Original tag machine.

competition, the Company developed strategies to come out ahead: it bought out competing businesses, added machinery, increased advertising and lowered prices while maintaining fine quality merchandise. Dennison developed the necessary expertise to overcome unfavorable circumstances.

Production and sales mushroomed over the next few years. In 1879 ninety million tags were sold. Dennison practically had a monopoly on the sale of shipping tags. In spite of tough competition, "It was perhaps the only concern known by everyone as Tag-makers."[11]

By 1882, patents for the shipping and the merchandise tags had both expired. This brought about the most severe competition that Dennison had ever experienced. E.W. thought the way to gain an advantage over his competitors was to begin production of a printed shipping tag. In the 1880s, he began testing this idea. First, he used a machine that made plain tags. Then, these plain tags were hand-fed into a second machine that did the printing. The concept was sound, but the process was time consuming, costly and inefficient.

Finally, in 1890, after much experimentation, the functions of the two machines were perfected and combined into one operation. This new innovative machine was markedly productive, capable of producing 20,000 printed tags per hour. It was so impressive that it was shown at the 1893 Chicago World's Fair.[12] Dennison's Mr. Issiah Taylor, proudly accompanied the machine to the Fair and demonstrated its capacity to scores of curious onlookers at Machinery Hall. While

World's Fair kiosk, 1893.

at the Fair, the shipping tag machine produced 200,000 tags a day! Also quite intriguing for fair goers to observe, was the ingenuity of the Company's machine for stringing Merchandise Tags.[13]

> Stringing tags was a cottage industry for Framingham families. In the early years, families received ten cents for each completed box, which contained 1,000 tags. Some years later, families received twenty cents per box. Ten dollars or more could be earned by a family each month.

To top off Dennison's mechanical inventiveness, a fanciful booth in the Manufactures and Liberal Arts Building showcased a treasure trove of merchandise that appeared in the Company's most recent Stationers' Catalogue. Produced specifically for this event and displayed on pages 55-56 of the catalogue, were four Chicago World's Fair napkins. The napkins were designed with views of eleven of the Fair's magnificent buildings, accompanied by descriptions. One napkin diagramed

YELLOWSTONE PARK TRANSPORTATION CO.
Property of

DENNISON MFG. CO.

DENNISON'S STANDARD

CHICAGO.

M

NOTICE TO PASSENGERS.
YELLOWSTONE PARK TRANSPORTATION CO. assumes no responsibility for hand baggage in charge of passengers While making the tour of the Park, see that your baggage is aboard your coach before starting on each day's journey. Every piece of baggage should have name and address of owner thereon.

Casa Verde
TEXAS VEGETABLES
AND
BERMUDA ONIONS
ROY CAMPBELL
WISE & WRIGHT, INC.
ROBSTOWN, TEXAS

SWEDISH AMERICAN LINE
PIER 97 NORTH RIVER
FOOT OF WEST 57TH ST. NEW YORK

NOT WANTED
DETACH IF WANTED ON VOYAGE

Julius Baer
CINCINNATI'S TELEGRAPH FLORIST
FLOWERS
DATE
RECEIVED BY--
To
No.
No.
43 EAST 4TH STREET • PHONE-MAIN-3662

Distinctive shipping tags.

Galvins ROSES,
124 Tremont St.
Boston.
For
SAMPLE PRINTED WITH 3 COLORS
WE GROW OUR OWN CUT FLOWERS AND PLANTS

the exposition grounds called Jackson Park — an ideal purchase for the trade and a perfect souvenir for the public.

It was not surprising that orders for the printed tags quickly outnumbered those for plain tags. Colorful tags, with distinctive characteristics, carried company trade names to merchants and the general public. They were like miniature billboards. This was advertising at its best! It was not costly and it got results. Dennison gradually worked toward the day when production would be a billion or more tags a year. That was more than fulfilled in 1920 when total production exceeded two billion tags.

In the 19th century, Dennison created their signature product, the Shipping Tag. By the 20th century, Dennison proved that this distinctive product could definitely stand the test of time.

GUMMED LABELS AND DECORATIVE SEALS

With the onset of the Civil War in 1861, Dennison & Company expanded and grew at a rapid pace.[14] This growth was the result of government contracts received by Dennison and additional business in New York, New Jersey and Pennsylvania. Accelerated expansion and prosperity inspired E.W. in his quest to manufacture and sell superior quality products as efficiently as possible. He began to feel certain that he was on the road to developing a thriving, successful, well-established business.

At this time, Dennison & Company was importing gummed labels from the Dondorf Company in Germany to add to its product line. These ordinary, popular labels were used by merchants to mark all types of products. As with other imported goods, the increased cost of the German gummed labels during wartime eventually made it prohibitive for Dennison to continue purchasing and offering them to customers.

E.W. still wanted to offer a gummed label to the American market. The need was there! At first he sought out a New York manufacturer of labels, but found their product wanting. Unable to find a quality American label to add to his offerings, a new challenge presented itself. The next important product, the gummed label, would be manufactured by Dennison & Company and added to the Stationers' Line. This was the beginning of a very lucrative seal and label business.

In 1865, two years after the shipping tag was patented, Dennison began to manufacture and offer the gummed label. E.W. called upon the artistry of William Stratton to create its design.

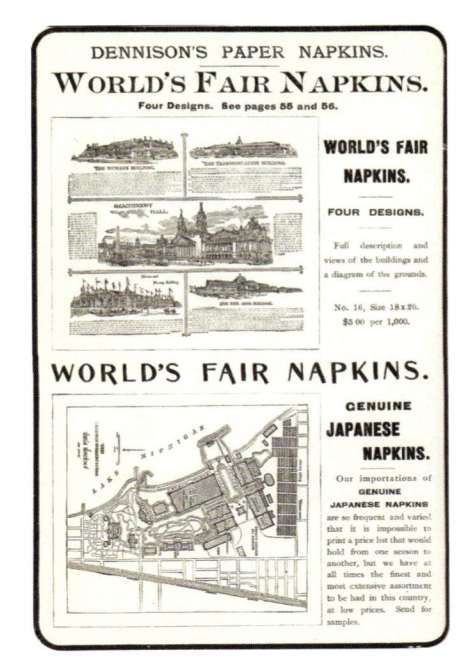

The perfect souvenir!

Stratton gummed labels.

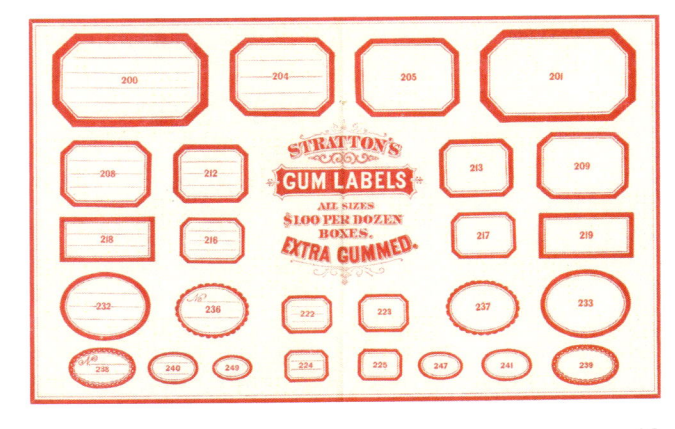

Hand gumming – *Blue Lantern slide.*

Stratton's finished plan was plain and simple: a white background with a distinctive red border. In the initial stages of label production, gumming of the paper was done by hand, until once again, inventive Mr. Stratton devised a means of accomplishing this task by machine. Machine gumming was exactly the addition needed to speed up production and meet rising demand. Each perfectly cut label, with its smooth writing surface was appropriate for marking all kinds of merchandise, making it "indispensable" to the tradesmen.

As sales increased, the plain labels were made to carry the buyer's trademark. At first they were printed in one color; very few illustrations were used. As the value of trademarks became apparent to merchants, they began to ask for specialty labels to complement their company products. Like the tags, customized, artistically designed gummed labels soon appeared. Merchants found a colorful unique paper label with their own trade name acted as a simple, inexpensive advertisement that attracted buyers to their

doorsteps. The labels did the selling!

William H. Trowbridge label. South Framingham, circa 1875.

From the very beginning, fine quality paper and superior gum were used to make sure the label stuck securely. The sticking quality had to be perfect! Dennison's Stratton Gummed Labels[15] which adhered quickly and permanently were perfect. This made

Artistically designed printed labels.

20

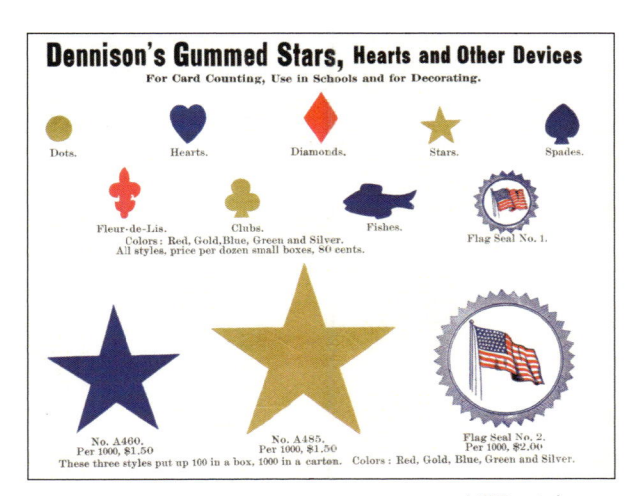

Dennison's Gummed Stars, Hearts and Other Devices
For Card Counting, Use in Schools and for Decorating.

Dots. Hearts. Diamonds. Stars. Spades.

Fleur-de-Lis. Clubs. Fishes. Flag Seal No. 1.
Colors: Red, Gold, Blue, Green and Silver.
All styles, price per dozen small boxes, 80 cents.

No. A460, No. A485, Flag Seal No. 2,
Per 1000, $1.50 Per 1000, $1.50 Per 1000, $2.00
These three styles put up 100 in a box, 1000 in a carton. Colors : Red, Gold, Blue, Green and Silver.

1899 catalogue.

them readily accepted and favored by the American market. Stratton's process of machine gumming for labels influenced the manufacture of one of Dennison's most important products for the future — gummed paper.

Eye stopper, 1949.

In 1865, a few thousand of the new gummed labels were sold. Into the 20th century, along with the common labels with the red border used by businesses and in the home, catalogues offered postal labels, gummed hearts, stars, numbers, animals, flowers, and all sorts of gummed decorations. Novelty seals and labels with new designs were added continually. Sales shot up into the millions! Dennison's gummed labels became the standard by which all other labels were to be judged.

DENNISON'S POSTAL LABELS. WHITE PAPER, BLUE INK.

From _____
POSTMASTER: Should for any reason this Package not be delivered to the party addressed we will send the necessary postage for its return, if you will kindly let us know the amount required.
To _____
Merchandise.
DENNISON MANUFACTURING CO—MAKERS—BOSTON, NEW YORK, PHILADELPHIA, CHICAGO, CINCINNATI, & ST.LOUIS.

In Stock, 50 in a box, as above, at $2.50 per 1000.
Or printed to order, with sender's address, 250 for $1.50, 500 for $2.00, 1000 for $3.00

Dennison Manufacturing Co.

"Nature" and Holiday Seals

Natural Colors
Used in kindergarten, primary and church schools for merit awards, to illustrate written work and for handicraft novelties.

Strongly Gummed
Very popular also for sealing gift packages, decorating price cards, signs, stationery, invitations, favors, costumes and tally, menu and place cards.

Bird Seals
No. B622 Robin (illustrated)
B623 Parrot
B624 Duckling
B625 Bluebird
B627 Chicken
B629 Bluebird (illustrated)
25 in a box   20 boxes in a carton
B628 Display carton of 50 small boxes, all designs (illustrated).

B622
B629

Floral Seals
No. F616 Red Rose   No. F618 Violet
F617 Chrysanthemum   F619 Pink Rose (illustrated)
25 in a box   20 boxes in a carton
F621 Display carton of 50 small boxes, all designs

F619

Butterfly Seals
No. B632 (Illustrated) 25 (5 designs assorted) in a box
20 boxes in a carton
B631 Display carton of 50 small boxes

B632
(5 Designs Asstd.)

P609 P419

V643
(2 Designs Asstd.)

H653

Holiday Seals
Designs of seals appropriate to each holiday and season are made for the three Dennison Holiday Lines,—Christmas, Spring Holidays (Valentine, St. Patrick, Patriotic and Easter) and Hallowe'en,—and listed in the holiday booklets and price lists. (See page 90.)

B628

S599 (2 Sizes Asstd.) E649 407

[60]

Nature and holiday seals, 1924 catalogue.

TISSUE AND CREPE PAPER

In 1871, Dennison imported white tissue paper from the Crompton Paper Company of Bury, England. This tissue paper, that would not tarnish jewelry or silverware, was added to the Jewelers' Line. Dennison also purchased colored tissue that was considered the ideal paper for arts and crafts.

Although this product sold, it was not until the 1880s that Dennison started to concentrate on ways to grow the tissue business. The Company's first effort occurred in 1881 with the creation of an Art Department in the Boston store. It appears that one young woman was hired to staff this new department. Her job was to fashion innovative items using the colored tissue and test its possibilities. The market for the white tissue had already been fixed. In order to draw attention to the potential of the colored tissue, a pamphlet called *The Uses of Tissue Paper*[16] was published in 1882. This little guide explained how the paper could be used to make flowers, lamp shades, doll clothes and other decorative items.

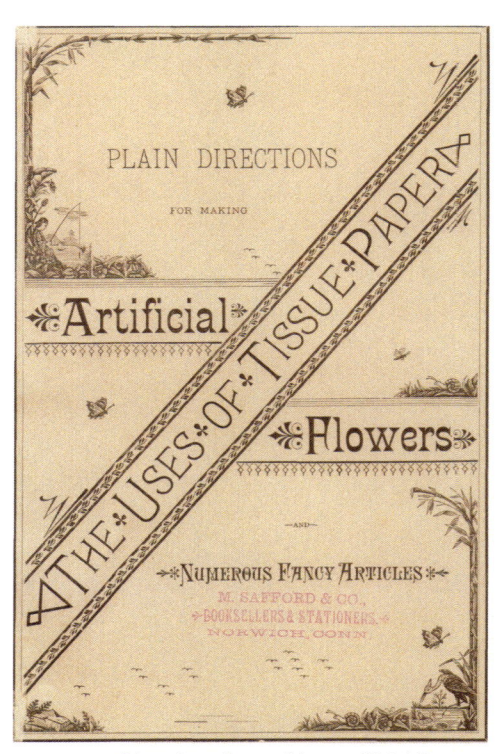

Directions for making artificial flowers and fancy articles, catalogue.

The catalogue of 1886-87 featured white tissue napkins and tablecloths. Page 50-51 offered "Dennison's Assortment of Materials for Tissue Paper Flowers," which was made available for the first time. Assortments included colored paper and accessories (wire, leaves, centers, petals etc.) for flower making. Wholesalers, who bought in large quantities, could buy the various individual items by the gross or dozens. Dennison also thought of the retailers who purchased merchandise in small amounts. For them, a "Beginner Outfit" was designed, which included all the materials needed to make one flower with a simple book of instructions. All the essentials were put into a convenient individual paper box. The flower kit was attractively presented in just the right way to entice the home crafter.

A most notable discovery occurred in the late 1880s when an English manufacturing company found that tissue paper could be crinkled. The crinkling was first done by hand and then later it was accomplished by machine. Crinkling added to the paper's artistic value, and made it more versatile. Dennison purchased the new crinkled paper and first advertised this interesting new import as "Crepe Tissue Paper" in its 1890 catalogue.

There appeared to be very little interest in crepe tissue paper until 1892, when a how-to demonstration was held in the Boston store. Mr. Ewing, sales manager for the New York district, had seen paper dolls beautifully designed and dressed by Mrs. Heath and her daughters of Buffalo, New York displayed in a small city store.[17] The artistry of the little dolls prompted him to suggest that Dennison invite the Heaths to show the practical and decorative uses of this new paper product in Boston. The women, who had successfully made and marketed a fanciful line of paper dolls, were certainly well aware of crepe paper's endless possibilities. Such an exciting and challenging opportunity could not be resisted by the three Heath sisters!

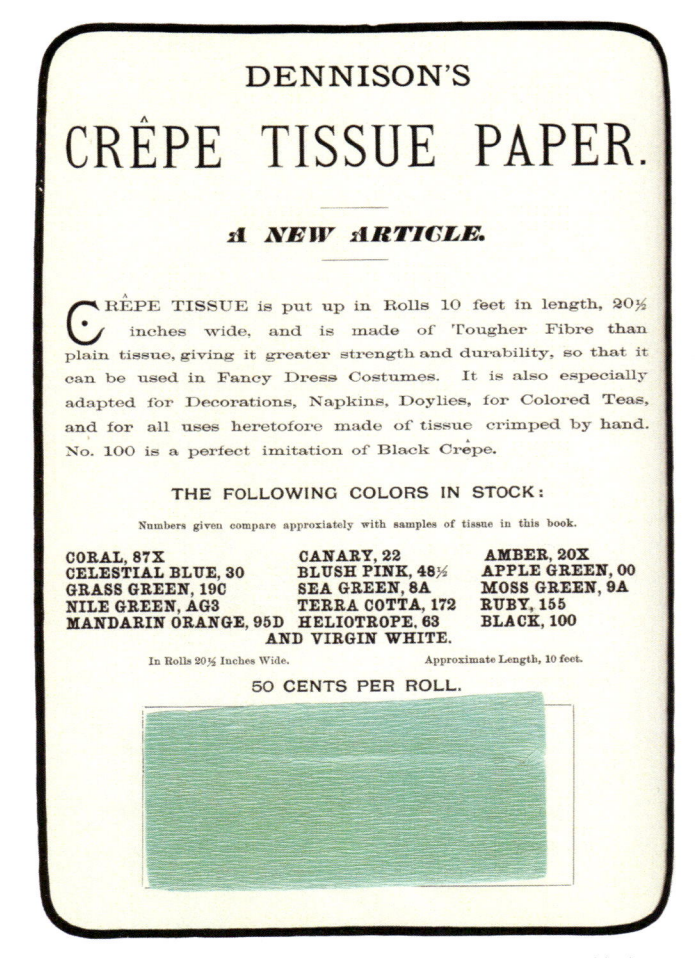

New crinkled paper, 1890 catalogue.

As Mr. Ewing walked past a small store in Buffalo, New York, he paused to look into one of the store's decorated windows. A collection of lovely paper dolls caught his attention. He stepped inside the store and spoke to a nearby saleswoman who told him that her mother, Mrs. Heath had made the dolls. Mr. Ewing purchased four of the paper dolls, which he sent to Mr. Dyer and Mr. Pope in the New York store. The men immediately saw the possibilities! Arrangements were made for Mrs. Heath to send additional samples to New York. Her samples included photo frames and candle shades as well as fancy dolls. These delightful novelties were sent to several of the Dennison stores where they sold so vigorously that Mrs. Heath was able to open a small factory. Later, Mrs. Heath visited Mr. Dyer in the New York store where an agreement was made. It was decided that Mrs. Heath's three daughters who were well-trained by their mother would be invited to the Boston store. They were to decorate the store and demonstrate the many aesthetic and novel uses of crepe paper to the store's visitors. – F.E. Ewing *Reminiscences*, July 7, 1914, 12-14.

Dennison's Franklin Street store.

On demonstration day, passengers in horse drawn carriages lined the roadside outside of the Dennison store. Curious onlookers exited their carriages and filed through the crowded Franklin Street entrance. They were instantly captivated. This soft velvety paper was magically transformed into roses and daffodils, doll costumes, and favors by Miss Mary Heath's nimble fingers. The crowd was bedazzled! News of the successful Boston demonstration traveled to the Dennison stores in New York, Philadelphia, Chicago, and St. Louis. The Heath sisters were a perfect fit. They were the thrust that created the appeal, which then propelled the sale of tissue and crepe paper into perpetual motion.

By 1894, annual sales of the imported crepe paper reached one million rolls. Booklets entitled *Tissue Paper Entertainment, Art and Decoration,* and *Art of Window Dressing with Dennison Crepe Paper Tissue* were published by the Company to promote sales. Crepe Paper innovation and products were definitely on the rise.

At the same time that Dennison was promoting crepe paper, department stores were just beginning to flourish. The growing crowds who attended the Dennison demonstrations eventually captured the attention of department store proprietors. Prompted by the public's enthusiasm for this new art form, the proprietors invited Dennison instructors to show the many creative uses of this increasingly popular product. The young ladies who were sent to these stores, not only offered intriguing demonstrations, but they

Miss Mary Heath.

Crepe paper innovations, 1899 booklet.

USE ONLY DENNISON'S IMPORTED CRÊPE AND TISSUE PAPER.

Dennison instructors, 1927.

also beautified the store with whimsical crepe paper decorations and surprises.

Now with a foot in the door, Dennison was able to place crepe paper, followed by other products into this new venue, and for the first time right into the consumer's hand.

Interest in the craft of tissue and crepe paper brought added attention to the concept of the Art Department. From the tiny Art Department created earlier in Boston, there was expansion to Dennison stores in other cities, which now drew interest from the public as well as the trades. The instructors educated the merchants and consumers in the many uses of crepe paper and other products. This was a perfect testing ground for new goods and ideas.

Rather than using ads that only appeared in directories for merchants, Dennison began to advertise in magazines such as, *The Ladies Home Journal, Youth's Companion, The Country Gentleman* and *The Saturday Evening Post.* The Company discovered the extraordinary value and return of advertising in a variety of journals and magazines that were bought and read by the general public. Dennison had come upon a wonderful new market — the Public — the Consumer!

Sunday Journal advertisement, November 4, 1928.

Women's Home Companion advertisement, September, 1911.

Shipping tag, 1912.

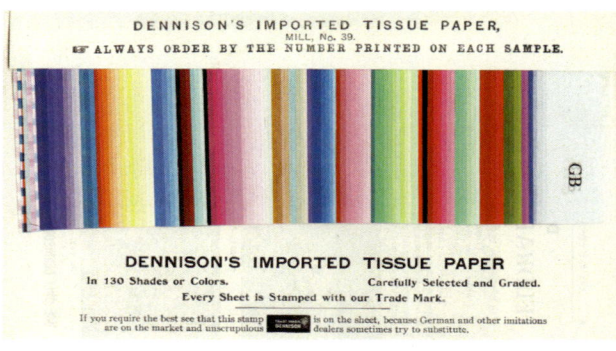

Art and decoration crepe chart, 1898.

Decorated crepe paper "folds," 1924.

On October 3, 1894, a most important development took place! After months of experimentation at the Roxbury plant, Dennison began to manufacture its own crepe paper — the first to be produced in America.[18] Before this time, all tissue and crepe paper advertised in the catalogues had been imported from Europe. The Company started with the production of its "Standard" plain crepe, which was introduced for the first time in the 1895 catalogue. By 1897, Dennison developed "Tinted Crepe" in twelve colors followed by printed or decorated crepe. "Imperial Crepe," was also added to the market in the same year. It was coarser, lighter in weight and stretched less than the "Standard" paper.[19]

Over time, one by one, new items were added to the line — napkins, fans, lunch sets, table covers, and, *oh so* many unique novelties. Perhaps a surprising addition is a crepe paper tea bag that was introduced in 1916. Ready-made items could be purchased for immediate use, or customers could buy enticing crepe paper "folds" and delight themselves to their own creations.

Unique novelties, 1924 and 1926.

The sale of imported crepe diminished by 50% as Dennison Crepe grew in popularity. By 1900, about three million rolls of crepe were produced each year. In 1914, a finer textured paper, superior to Imperial, was introduced to the world. This refined crepe product called "Dennison Crepe," had qualities that were similar to those of fabric. Catalogues in the 1920s stated that this crepe, due to its strength, could be sewn by hand or machine — it could be "shirred, tucked and ruffled without tearing." This sounded perfect for fashions, costumes and hats. And perfect it was!

Thousands flocked to the Dennison Stores in New York, Chicago, Philadelphia and Boston for Costume Show Week in the spring of 1924.[20] Artistically designed crepe paper hats and dresses modeled by store employees, showed the possibilities of creating the "exceptional" in party apparel. Fashions were magically presented in stories like Aladdin or Mother Goose, or in themes such as the seasons, holidays and sweet treats. Two little girls in Chicago caused quite a stir dressed as the Wrigley Spearmint Twins, complete with the familiar stick of chewing gum in hand. The grand finale in Boston was a charming costume that included all thirty-five colors of "Dennison Crepe." Of course there was that healthy bit of rivalry to see which store could present the best costume display.

The Fashion Show

These are some of the young ladies who acted as models in the annual "Fashion Show" held this month in the Chicago Store.

Chicago costume show, 1922.

We cordially invite you and your friends to our Annual
CREPE PAPER COSTUME SHOW
April 25 to May 2, inclusive
12.30 to 2.30 DAILY
Dennison's
26 FRANKLIN STREET, BOSTON

Advertisement in the *Boston Globe,* January 10, 1923. Exhibition of party crepe paper costumes at Jordan Marsh Company, Boston store.

Crepe paper costume show invitation, Dennison's Boston store, 1925.

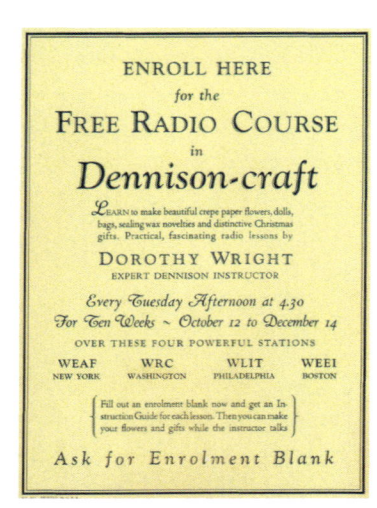

Afternoon radio "talks," 1926.

Well aware of new technology, Dennison took advantage of the radio as a far-reaching vehicle for advertising. In the spring of 1925, the Company aired its first radio course. Miss Rusk, of the New York store, presented a crepe paper flower making course from station WJZ in New York City. Prior to the ten part series, listeners were offered a free instruction guide and were told what crepe paper materials to have on hand for each lesson. More than one thousand guides were requested. Listeners eagerly purchased the necessary materials to prepare for the afternoon "radio talks." The course was an instant hit! Many letters were received from women who enjoyed the practical and decorative aspects of the lessons that the program provided. These enthusiastic radio fans inspired Dennison to offer courses from well-known stations in Boston (WEEI), Philadelphia (WLIT), Washington (WRC), and New York (WEAF) the following year.[21] By the late 1920s, dealers from Seattle to Boston made arrangements with stations to broadcast Craft Talks to their listeners on a regular schedule.

Enter the "Golden Age" of film making. Lights, Camera, Action! These words echoed from director Ramsdell in July of 1926 as Dennison began filming, "Putting the Win in Windows." This short silent movie was meant to acquaint business organizations with the attractive uses of crepe paper in window displays. When the film was presented, a salesman was available to offer decorating information and

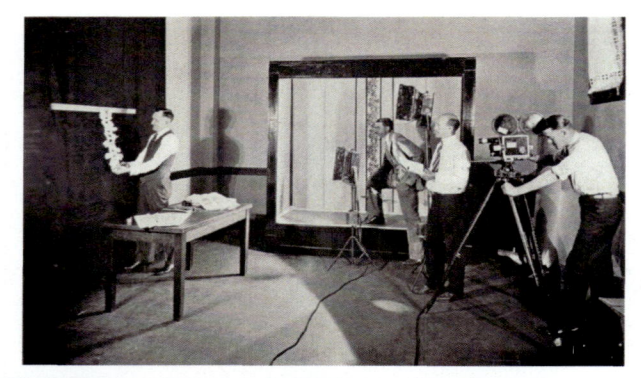

Director Ramsdell filming interior scene for "Putting the Win in Windows" at Dennison Manufacturing Company factory, 1926.

A studio was set up in the back of the Display Room at the Framingham Plant to film the interior scenes of "Putting the Win in Windows." The exterior scenes were mostly taken in Framingham. Two downtown shops, Ahearns Stationery Store and Bates and Holdsworth, displayed enticing windows with artistic backgrounds and decorations created from Dennison products to show off their windows for the filming.

Movies that advertised Company products to attract the public were also filmed and shown in movie theatres. An article in the 1919 *Round Robin*, mentions one thousand feet of film featuring Dennison goods and crafts produced by Prisma Motion Picture "appearing at only the best theatres." The St. George Theatre, on Concord Street in downtown Framingham was one of the many "best theatres" that showed this film clip.

Exterior scenes were filmed on Concord Street in Framingham near the railroad crossing.

advice as the scenes unfolded on the screen. Surely, goods set in a beautifully appointed window would cause passers-by to flock into the store to make purchases!

We mustn't forget the telephone! Dennison praised the use of this technology. The phone was a reliable way for the shopkeeper to reach directly into a home or business. It was a quick and easy source of advertising with a personal touch. Dennison suggested a local stationer or shop owner might telephone the person in charge of planning a party, dance, or social function and offer helpful decorating ideas.[22] Perhaps suggestions from the *Party Magazine* or the how-to booklet, *How to Decorate Halls, Booths, and Automobiles* might be exactly what the planner would need to achieve a distinct party atmosphere. This informative conversation could be closed with an

Party Magazine, 1927.

Parade automobile decorated with Dennison crepe paper, 1914.

invitation for the prospective customer to visit the store. During the visit, the shop owner could point out unique Dennison ideas and products available to design a welcoming special occasion. Chances are the "potential customer" would become a "buying customer."

With the introduction of crepe paper, Dennison took a revolutionary step in merchandising. Its crepe paper demonstrations, the creation of how-to booklets, the formation of Art Departments, the expansion of magazine advertising, the appearance of the Company's products in retail department stores, and the use of technological advances brought the name of Dennison from the commercial world into the home. This offered limitless opportunities for the new fancy paper.

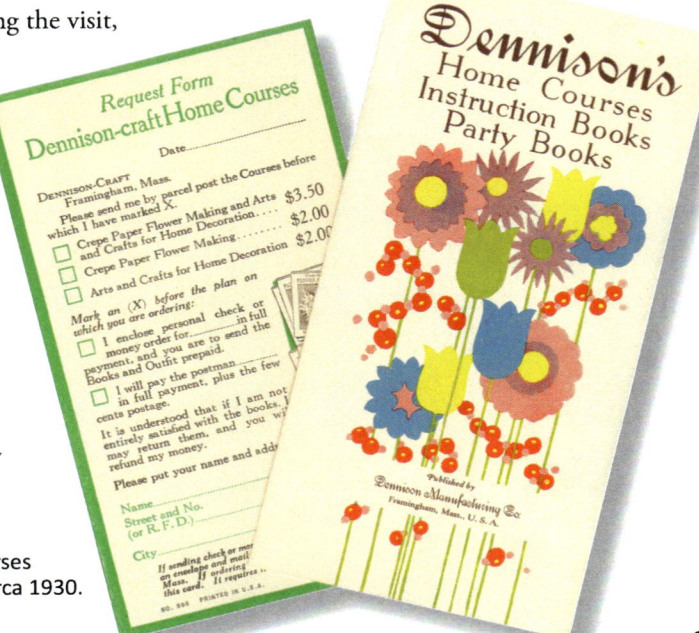

Dennison home courses instruction books, circa 1930.

SEALING WAX FOR HOME AND OFFICE

When we hear the words sealing wax, it might bring to mind royals and monarchs who used wax to seal important documents and papers during the Renaissance or the Middle Ages. However, in the centuries that followed, businesses and professions continued to seal important packages and papers with a distinctive monogram or trademark.

Dennison's sealing wax business developed when the Company found its supply source no longer offered a consistent high quality product. As with other products, Dennison wanted to continue to offer a superior sealing wax to its customers. In 1879, with this tradition in mind, Dennison Manufacturing Company opened its own sealing wax factory in Brooklyn, New York. At about the same time as Dennison was seriously drawing attention to its line of crepe and tissue, a line of sealing wax was launched and advertised in the catalogues of the 1880s.

The Only Factory In The World Devoted Exclusively To The Manufacture Of Sealing Wax.

An eight page booklet published in 1884 entitled *Dennison Sealing Wax Factory,* featured a picture of the factory in Brooklyn, New York on its cover. Beneath the picture was the caption, "The Only Factory In The World Devoted Exclusively To The Manufacture Of Sealing Wax." This little booklet described the finest perfumed sealing wax in twenty colors, and elegantly engraved seals with graceful ebony, rosewood and horn handles. Also included was an instruction page called *The Art of Sealing a Letter,* which offered this advice: "there is great art in sealing a letter … The taper, the stick of wax and daintily engraved seal are now requisites of the fashionable writing table." To whom might this perfumed wax and these fancy seals appeal? According to the booklet, "All ladies who wish to be in the *mode* now use Sealing Wax in their correspondence." Who could resist a fancy little design on the back

Perfumed sealing wax tray, 1886.

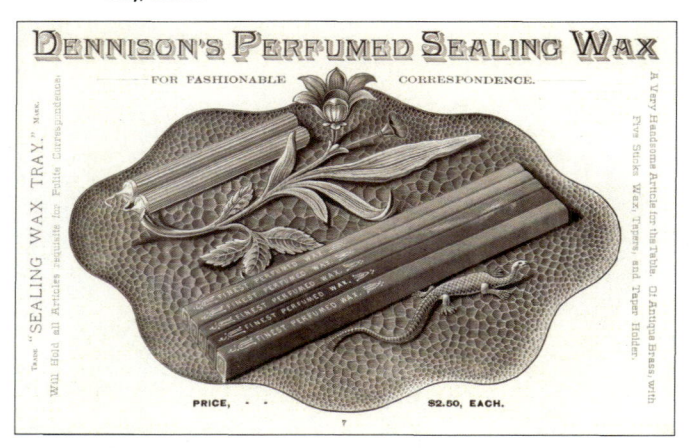

Ladies in the *mode,* 1924 Dennison catalogue.

of a personal letter! Sealing wax dressed one's letter properly and granted it the dignity that it certainly deserved. Dennison advised the owner of a stationery shop that sealing wax and its accessories would be very appealing if they were featured in his shop.

In the mid-1890s, the Smithsonian Institute in Washington featured an exhibition of Dennison's sealing wax. Thirty years later, the Company replaced this first display. The new exhibition included novelties made from, or decorated with sealing wax, as well as information on sealing wax basics. The October, 1924 issue of *Round Robin,* an informative publication for Dennison employees, encouraged its readers who would be visiting the Washington area to drop into the Smithsonian and enjoy this exceptional new exhibit. The article also claimed that the sealing wax exhibit was considered one of the most beautiful displays at the Institute.

The ancient custom of utilizing sealing wax for letters and documents continued well into the 20th century. Along with commercial uses, its vibrant colors led to the ongoing development of many innovative and aesthetic uses.

There was always something *new* just around the corner. Dennison had a great way of getting the word out about its new products in a little magazine called *What Next?*[23] This bimonthly publication was designed and written to help shopkeepers promote Dennison products. It featured helpful pointers for advertising and increasing the sale of sealing wax in its 1924 autumn edition. This issue offered attractively prepared ads for the promotion of sealing wax meant to be used by shopkeepers in their own locales. A sample of proposals included a lantern slide for theatre advertising that would feature the store's name and address, an editorial that could be printed in the local paper, and a radio talk on the many uses of sealing wax.

Commercial Sealing Wax has a steady demand from business houses, banks, etc.

1926 Dennison catalogue.

According to the October 1924 *Round Robin,* "the term Round Robin has come to apply to any document circulated among a number of readers, each of whom is supposed to contribute something to it."

The first *Round Robin* was written by Henry S. Dennison and published in September, 1908. Mr. Dennison referred to this first edition as "Chirp the First." It contained what he called "shop talk." Each issue of the magazine would offer an opportunity to "talk it over." Information that was included came from the "selling force" and the "working force." Articles "talked" about everyday selling experiences, the variety of goods, and the quality and features of the merchandise produced. Over time, as the Company grew, the audience and topics broadened. Factory and district news was always of first importance. Other articles that were included could be social, educational, informational, or just for fun. The Smithsonian reference is an example of information that might be included in a *Round Robin.* All the issues were filled with pictures. Mr. Dennison saw his employees as family, "and this was a way to let the family know what was happening. Each has a share in the work which is being done for all." *Round Robin* was last published in 1930.

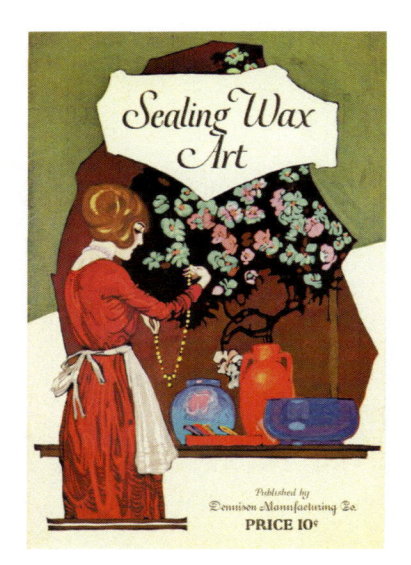

Sealing Wax Art, 1922.

Sealing Wax Craft, 1932.

These so called "helps" were sent to merchants upon request, ready-made by Dennison, and just right for local advertisement. So many "gentle" suggestions were meant to free up the customers purse strings!

Catalogues of the 1920s advertised Wax Craft as the art of molding, decorating and painting with wax — an art that was easily learned. Items such as Wax Sets, Wax Craft Outfits and tools were advertised as "a splendid gift" for wax art work. To pique the publics' interest in this blossoming new art form, dealers offered craft classes and demonstrations

Promotional advertising, *What Next?,* 1924.

in their stores. A twenty-four page illustrated book, *Sealing Wax Art,* sold for ten cents, and gave instructions for fashioning unusual things like earrings, pendants and compacts. The 1924 Christmas issue of the *Ladies' Home Journal* advertised *Sealing Wax Art* as "a book that offers you literally scores of suggestions for original gifts, for charming and useful gifts, doubly welcome because you made them."

As Wax Craft was popularized, the sale of wax, accessory items and wax for commercial use increased, and became quite profitable. Fanciful three dimensional creations, in brilliant colors, were so appealing to the eye! With the use of vivid imagination, the novelties that could be fashioned took off, and the possibilities were found to be boundless. Charming lampshades, candlesticks, boxes, vases and figures were among the many inventions. Sealing Wax, like crepe paper, was a product that was perfect for art and craft work.

The thirty-six colors of Dennison Wax make possible a great variety of beautiful effects. The numbers with the prefix number "2" are those in which the Letter Size is made. The prefix number "3" indicates the De Luxe Size

Sealing Wax Craft, 1925.

Although crepe paper was well known, when combined with sealing wax, the two became a most attractive drawing card, appealing to the home consumer. Together, crepe paper and sealing wax was the energizer that turned Dennison's attention from not only selling to wholesalers and retailers, but to the general public as well. The Company was moving in a new dimension. Crepe Paper and Sealing Wax were Dennison's first non-commercial products. Both were skillfully designed to entice the Lady of the House! *What Next?*

The Holiday Line: *A Novel Idea!*

The Holiday Line was the brainchild of Dennison Manufacturing Company, the first American company to develop and manufacture holiday products.[1] Historian Charlotte Heath stated in her 1928 study, *The Christmas Line,* "It is commonly thought of as having begun with the first Christmas tag in 1901, but like most things, its roots extend farther back than is first apparent."[2]

THE PATRIOTIC LINE

The Holiday Line was a natural outgrowth of the Company's early foundation products. Dennison drew from goods that were already available and then customized them for each holiday. For example, in the 1890s items such flag napkins, paper flags, and red, white and blue striped tissue paper and garlands were advertised in dealer catalogues for general use. These basic products were then styled specifically for Memorial Day, Washington's Birthday and the Fourth of July, and became the perfect showcase to launch the Patriotic Line.

As Patriotic items were popularized, Dennison thoughtfully designed its merchandise and built the Line with the events and the trends of the time in mind. Linking product to event proved to be a wise and profitable strategy.[3] During the Spanish American War of 1898, this approach was very apparent in the merchandise that was offered. According to Charlotte Heath, early "correspondence mentions a crude American flag seal which sold enormously during the war, and a broadside advertises Patriotic crepe in a 'Remember the Maine' design."[4] Dennison also produced an embossed red

136   DENNISON MANUFACTURING COMPANY,

DENNISON'S STANDARD CRÊPE PAPER.
PRINTED PATRIOTIC DESIGNS.
10 ft. lengths, 20½ in. wide, in handsome illuminated boxes. In beautiful colors of Red, White and Blue.

RED, WHITE AND BLUE STRIPED.

No. P721. Red, White and Blue Striped .... Trade Price, per Box, 20 cents net.

AMERICAN FLAG DESIGN.

No. P725. American Flag Design .... Trade Price, per Box, 20 cents net.

AMERICAN FLAG DESIGN.

No. P728. American Flag, showing seven times on the length   Trade Price, per Box, 20 cents net.
For Paper American Flags, see page 108.   For Red, White and Blue Tissue Paper, see page 146. Red, White and Blue Garlands illustrated on page 142.

Tags and Stationers' Specialties Catalogue,
1898 printed patriotic designs.

and black Admiral Dewey seal to honor the Admiral's return after the victory at Manila Bay. This seal was quite a success! Heath's Study noted, "Eight or nine hundred dozen boxes a day were sold at $1.00 per dozen, of which $.80 was profit."[5] From this humble "Patriotic" beginning, the Holiday Lines evolved over the next few years.

THE CHRISTMAS LINE

The seeds of the Christmas Line appeared in the latter part of the 1800s. A few products like red and green garland, decorated crepe paper and napkins designed specifically for Christmas first appeared in the 1898 catalogue. Merchandise from the Jewelers' and Stationers' Lines such as candy boxes, sealing wax sets, tissue paper outfits and handy boxes[6] had often been sold as gifts. It was about 1900 when these items along with others were grouped together and featured as "Christmas Gifts."

Although a scant number of Christmas items were available, it was in 1901 that Dennison took a "giant leap" forward. This was the year that the Company introduced its first explicitly new printed item, a tag to be used on Christmas packages. A once ordinary white shipping tag was now dressed up with flowing sprays of green holly. Simple, but distinctively original!

The following year, two new designs were added: a full-bearded Santa Claus and a tag with bells. The new holiday tags were described in the 1902 catalogue as: "Appropriate for the Christmas season. The use of these lends significance, and gives a finishing touch to the gift."

Christmas tags, 1901 and 1902.

Victory Crepe Paper World War I, December 14, 1918.

It was almost by accident that the holly seal made its entrance in 1902. An envelope of Christmas tags, secured with a holly seal was sent from the New York Store to the Boston store. Upon arrival, this unfamiliar little "sticker" drew immediate attention. In response to the positive attention the seal received, it was quickly manufactured for the upcoming Christmas season.[7]

At first, none of the Boston dealers showed any interest in this new festive holiday item. In order to draw attention to the holly seal, Dennison salesman, Mr. James Armington,[8] came up with this clever notion:

"I stayed on the floor in the [Boston] store at Christmastime, passing out the seals and putting the 10 cents in the box in front of me. And then what happened? Everybody wanted them. How many can you give us? How quick can we have them?"[9]

For a period of time, holly seals outsold the Christmas tags. This simple, ingenious marketing strategy equaled success!

Eye-catching multi-colored designs and embossing were added in 1904 to further entice buyers. These items were a definite hit! Each year imaginative new products were introduced. As a result, 1909 was referred to as a "banner year" for the Christmas Line. The early items, first sold through Dennison retail stores and a few wholesalers, proved to be very popular. Like other Dennison products, once these holiday goods were in the hands of the public, the Line flourished.

Holiday merriment and the Dennison name soon became inseparably linked. Retailers and consumers eagerly awaited the special seasonal products and the annual how-to *Christmas Book* in order to fashion their own holiday delights. Fancy seals, coin boxes, napkins, wrapping paper, cards, "Do Not Open" labels, crepe paper decorations, and streamers were just a few samples of the many festive Christmas items introduced. Quality products, handsome packaging, and a cleverly conceived marketing approach made Christmas Dennison's number one Line!

Christmas Book, 1924.

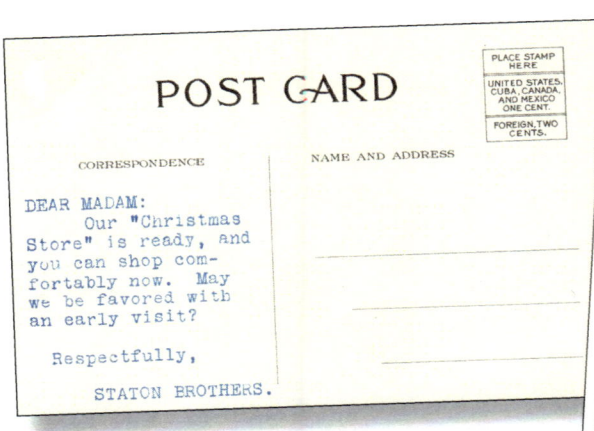

Artistically designed promotional cards sent to customers by shopkeepers.

As the Holiday Lines evolved, it was clear that their success was dependent upon a constant flow of original ideas. Dennison sought out talented and well-known artists[10] who could offer "new-fashioned" sketches and designs to create distinctive Holiday Lines. The Company also kept the familiar designs of the past that proved to be so appealing to the public.[11]

THE HALLOWEEN LINE

"Who popularized Hallowe'en?" asked Mr. Armington as he spoke before a 1916 salesman's class. *Dennison,* of course! According to Mr. Armington, "this holiday was losing its zest till about 1908 when Dennison started resuscitating it."[12]

The Company first took on the Halloween challenge with the introduction of the *Bogie Book* in 1909.[13] This whimsical Halloween booklet, introduced hostesses to party menus, games, and fanciful decorations that could be easily made from Dennison's paper products. It also included a handy price list of autumn merchandise that fit right in with the season. The first *Bogie Book* offered to retailers and home consumers was an easy sell. Its popularity was credited with much of the attention that Halloween then began to receive.

With interest aroused, Dennison focused more on the development of its Halloween Line in 1911. Four new seals, three silhouettes and a cutout were added to the fall catalogue. The second *Bogie Book* published in 1912 featured spooky

Bogie Book, 1925.

Halloween and Thanksgiving decorations pricelist, 1930.

The pumpkin man is made of cardboard covered with shaggy crepe paper moss. A couple of tiny tacks hold him erect.

poems, an eerie ghost story and costumes, along with entertainment, food, and magical party ideas. The *Bogie Book,* full of fun and folly, became an eagerly awaited annual holiday publication.

Halloween product offerings continued to increase — wispy witches in flight, plump orange pumpkins, sleepy-eyed bats, hump-backed cats … and luminous yellow moons. Dennison catalogues of the 1920s claimed that the Halloween Line offered every accessory needed for the *ideal* party. Bright, unique designs and products would provide that extra glow to this "spirited" holiday celebration — everything needed for a few good *shivers!*

For Company employees, the October issue of *Round Robin* featured Halloween party ideas. Old fashioned fun like the game of "Ghosts" or "Bobbing for apples," along with instructions for new games were found among the suggestions. The "Cheshire Cat Grin," challenged contestants to put on their widest grin while the "Official Measurer" and his assistant decided which broad smile would be worthy of the grand prize. In September of 1925, *Round Robin* declared that the Halloween Line had grown "to be of importance second only to Christmas."

VALENTINE'S DAY, ST. PATRICK'S DAY AND EASTER LINES

The Valentine's Day, St. Patrick's Day and the Easter Lines evolved in the same manner as the Christmas Line. Eventually, merchandise from these three holidays was combined with goods used for Patriotic occasions to form the "Spring" Line. The Spring, Halloween and Christmas Holiday Lines continued to grow in beauty and popularity. It might even be argued by some, or perhaps many, that the most enchanting Dennison products could be found in the Holiday Lines!

Just as the first Shipping Tag drew attention to the Dennison name in the business world, the Holiday Lines also offered an advertising bonus. These popular specialty products carried the Dennison name right into the homes of consumers, who then sought out the stores where these festive products were sold. While holiday

Saint Patrick's Day holiday table, 1920.

Valentine Outfit cover, 1915.

shoppers browsed, their attention was easily drawn to a tempting array of additional Dennison products displayed in the store. As a result, customers made more purchases and merchants showed more interest in stocking their shelves with a variety of Dennison goods. The public and the Trade were delighted.

Dennison created the product and the demand! Joyful holiday items embellished seasonal celebrations and offered tidings of good cheer. *Round Robin* in a resounding *chirp* proclaimed, "Wherever the holiday spirit presides — at a dance, at a party or at other festive occasions — there will be found Dennison holiday goods doing their part to make the occasion a merrier one." [14]

Dennison Easter cut-outs.

1928 catalogue.

39

The Next Step: *Transition*

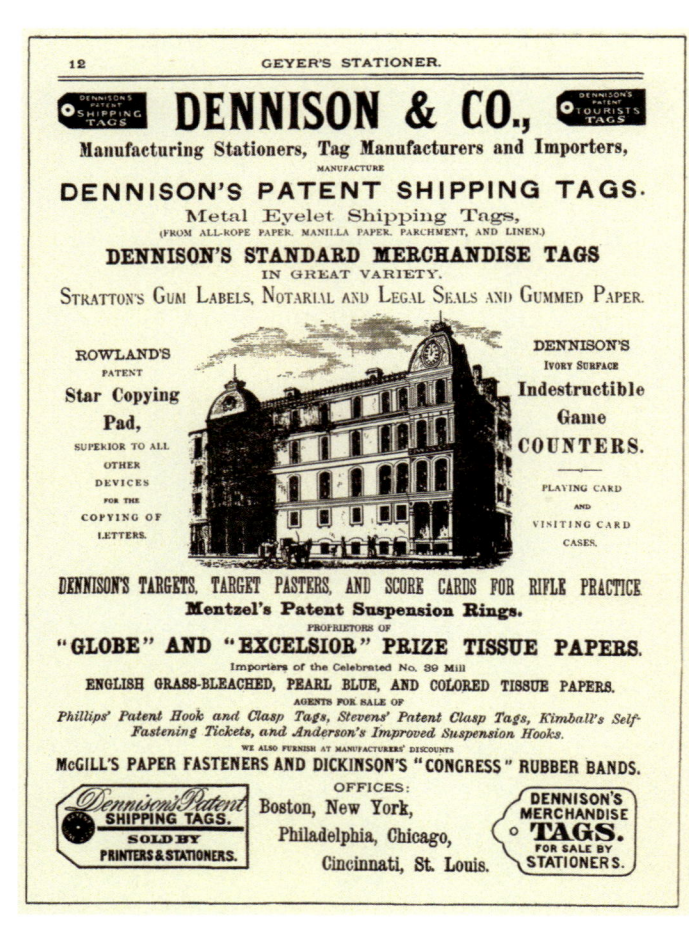

Dennison specialties advertised in *Geyer's Stationer* for 1877.

E.W. found that business conditions tended to fluctuate, especially after the Civil War. Despite these many ups and downs, by the final quarter of the 19th century, Dennison sales rose substantially with a notable profit. An outstanding volume of new marketable merchandise now became available. The trend was definitely upward!

In 1874, upon reflecting back on twenty-five years of successful business, E.W. recalled his father, Andrew's early words, "Whatever is worth doing at all is worth doing well," and his instructions "to first learn well, and then to work quickly." E.W. concluded, "Always acting in business on this maxim and these instructions, I believe contributed more toward our success than any one policy."[1] The Company could not only look back, but at the same time, proudly pave its way forward into the 20th century, with its foundation products solidly in place: boxes, tags, labels, crepe paper and sealing wax.

From the beginning Dennison & Company always kept a keen eye focused on the addition of new merchandise. Machines were devised as needed, and improved upon to keep up production and meet increasing sales volume. Through accident and design, Dennison mastered the power of advertising. Getting the word out about products was so profitable, that Dennison hired its first advertising man in 1901. The Company established a noticeable presence

Dennison goods travel the world!

throughout the United States. Goods were in the hands of merchants from east to west. Sales territories were developed and centered in cities beyond Boston — New York, Chicago, St. Louis, Philadelphia and Cincinnati. Each city had a branch store that offered goods to wholesalers, retailers and eventually to the public. With the success of the U.S. stores, the Company reached further out into the foreign market: Canada, Cuba, Central and South America, Australia and England. Dennison merchandise began to travel the world!

In 1882, sales finally reached the million dollar mark. Stores and offices continued to expand at home and abroad.

Dennison abroad – London.

*I will run in to see you on or about _____ 191_*
Henry G. Billinge.

While business was at the height of its greatest growth, E.W.'s health began to fail. Always keeping the future of the Company in sight, he began to organize his Company in order to ensure its future continuity and development. By the early 1880s, E.W. was no longer able to take the active leadership role that he had joyfully shouldered for so many years. As a result, in early 1886, he turned the presidency over to his older son, Henry B. Dennison. On September 22, of the same year, the man who successfully envisioned unlimited business possibilities for Dennison Manufacturing Company, quietly passed away. His work was done.[2]

The December 1919 *Round Robin,* featured an article entitled E.W. Dennison, which expressed E.W.'s character with these words:

"He had a vision of the Dennison Manufacturing Co. of 1919, because he knew the business would grow and grow if he and 'his boys' were honest in all their dealings, wide awake as to opportunities, and mindful always of quality. He followed his ideals through life and left his impress upon those who followed him."

The article also included a tribute from a pastor's recent sermon that praised E.W. as a solid citizen, a modest unassuming, public servant, a character who influenced others:

"This man was not a statesman. Nor was he a soldier or a man of letters. His contribution lay in the quality of his citizenship and in his industrial vision... In other words here was a successful businessman who was an idealist and also a man of action, a lover of his kind who put into practice his beliefs in social justice and democracy in industry."

Production quickly expanded well beyond the early days at the Dennison homestead in Maine as goods were sought after by dealers for their superior quality and value. Products from the Jewelers' and Stationers' Lines were manufactured at plants in Roxbury, Massachusetts, Brunswick, Maine, Brooklyn, New York, and at times in small local facilities like Newtonville, Massachusetts. Branch stores in Chicago and St. Louis had the know-how, and the machinery to produce shipping labels at their own facilities.

By the 1890s, the momentum of rapidly launching one desirable product after another, brought most of Dennison's production to its Roxbury plant and finally to a very spacious plant in South Framingham. On March 27, 1896, Dennison Manufacturing Company bought the factory that had previously housed the Para Rubber Company at Howard and Bishop Streets. While the Roxbury plant continued manufacturing operations, Dennison began the transition to its new Framingham quarters in 1897.

Factory of the Dennison Manufacturing Company, Roxbury, Massachusetts, 1894.

The Business Climate: *Nineteenth Century Framingham*

By the middle of the 19th century, three areas of Framingham, referred to as the villages, had developed. Each had its own distinct character. Saxonville was known for its mills and textiles, the Centre for its civic institutions, and South Framingham for its industry.

As the country recovered from the Civil War, South Framingham became a very appealing location for new industry. At the center of this blossoming business community was the railroad. Its importance began in 1834, when the "Yankee," a Boston and Worcester locomotive, trumpeted its approach to Framingham with its high pitched whistle and billowing clouds. The excited crowd lined the track in anticipation to welcome the arrival of the town's first train. An engine, with seven cars on wheels that resembled stagecoaches, chugged along the track and prepared to stop at Framingham's little depot. The train stopped momentarily as important passengers, including Governor John Davis and former Governor Levi Lincoln[1] boarded the train that headed toward the final destination, Unionville.[2] What an impact that first train had! From its very humble beginning, the railroad was destined to become the

The fare for these early trains from Framingham to Boston was $.75 in the summer and $1.00 in the winter. In the 1840s and 1850s track and spur lines were set to connect other parts of Framingham and area towns to South Framingham's center.

Simpson's Mill, Saxonville.

Memorial Library, Framingham Centre.

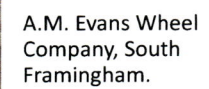

A.M. Evans Wheel Company, South Framingham.

South Framingham,
west of Concord Street.

gateway for new business opportunities in South Framingham.

The Civil War had proved the necessity and the value of speedy transportation. After the War, in order to service that growing need, railroad construction expanded throughout the United States. During the 1860s and 1870s, the explosion of new track brought an increasing number of passengers and freight trains in and out of Framingham every day. Its depot was a busy and exciting place! The Boston & Albany and Old Colony Rail lines, which now diverged in six directions, certainly became a business attraction and advantage. Around the bustling railroad station, buildings were erected and soon filled with new establishments: livery stables to transport passengers and baggage; the local newspaper, the *Framingham Gazette;*

Union block on
Waverley Street,
home of the
Framingham Gazette.

the first district court house; and a variety of shops were among the many enterprises that were meant to attract the public as well as businesses to this part of the village.

With the railroad well established in South Framingham, two exemplary companies arrived in the early 1880s. In 1882, the Bridges and Company boot and shoe factory, originally from Hopkinton, built a large impressive factory on the west side of South Framingham in the area of Farm Pond. The neighborhood that developed around the factory was named Coburnville after one of the factory partners. Coburnville had a school, a general store, and a hotel called The Coburn House.

Coburnville.

About the same time, the Para Rubber Shoe Company, the town's first connection to Brazil, settled in South Framingham. The company made every day and fashionable rubber footwear using high quality India rubber (natural rubber) from Para, Brazil. Their plant was located on the east side of South Framingham on the Boston & Albany Railroad line and was housed in "a triangular complex of wood and brick buildings surrounding a powerhouse with a tall smokestack. It was built by a group of local businessmen at a cost of $101,000 for the purpose of *luring* a new Boston venture out to Framingham."[3] Three neighborhoods for the Para workers grew up around the factory. Close to the triangular complex was the area known as the Para District; Lockerville was near the Natick line; and a little village in Sherborn was known as Sherbornville. Similar to Coburnville, these small

Para Rubber Shoe Company.

communities had their own amenities. By the close of the 1880s, the Para factory employed approximately 1,000 men and woman and produced 14,000 pairs of shoes each day.

Into the 1880s and 1890s, South Framingham continued to expand along the tracks. By 1890, the population grew from 4,665 to 9,500.[4] Most of the growth had taken place in South Framingham. Expansion and growth generated fresh ideas and vast changes. It was an exciting time, a time of many fascinating new conveniences: telephone services, indoor plumbing, sewerage, electric lights, hotels, banks, a theatre, new businesses and road improvements.

Reconstruction of roadways with smooth gravel services brought the privately owned Union Street Railroad Company to set track along the main streets of Union Avenue, Concord Street and Howard Street, in order to accommodate horse drawn cars in 1888. These street railway cars were meant to transport workers to their jobs, and to bring shoppers to savor the many charms of South Framingham's enterprising center. A few years later, the horse drawn cars were replaced with the electric trolley. Electric trolleys became a familiar sight in the area for the next thirty years. By 1890, there was an impressive new stone railroad station designed by noted architect Henry H. Richardson, two freight yards, and a roundhouse. Now, as many

Electric trolley, 1890s.

South Framingham Railroad Station.

Concord Street crossing, South Framingham.

as one hundred trains rumbled over the interconnected tracks carrying freight and passengers every day.

With so many people living, working and shopping in Framingham, a hospital was the next logical step. To accommodate the town's health care needs, the first hospital, the Framingham Emergency Hospital and Training School, was created in a home on Winthrop Street in 1893. This little two bed hospital was quickly outgrown. In 1898, a new Framingham hospital was built on Evergreen Street near Learned Pond where there was room for future growth and improvement.

As businesses and services were creating a new town center, it was decided that Town Meeting would be moved from Village Hall in Framingham Centre to South Framingham where it eventually held meetings at Waverley Hall. Town Government soon followed and took offices on the second floor of the Tribune Building.

Rear entrance to Framingham Hospital, South Framingham.

Waverley Building, corner of Waverley Street and Irving Square – South Framingham's first commercial block building, circa 1850.

Nobscot Building, located on the corner of Concord and Howard Street – commercial block built in 1871.

Framingham had weathered many ups and downs throughout the years. Now, as South Framingham's economy was flourishing, the tide was about to shift and change. The country was on the brink of economic hardship. Framingham was not to escape this fate. Two prominent plants, the Bridges factory and the Para Rubber Company, both troubled by financial and organizational problems, closed their doors in 1891. Other local factories and businesses were cutting back, causing hundreds of workers to lose their jobs.

In an attempt to boost business, small companies developed.[5] One of these, The Hickory Wheel Company, moved into a section of the Para Rubber plant with fifty workers to manufacture bicycles. In spite of many creative attempts, business in Framingham and throughout the country took a downturn in 1893. This trend, known as the Panic of '93, became the worst depression of the 19th century and was problematic for the next four years. Seeing no end in sight, Framingham businessmen knew that something must be done. Thereupon "the leading business and civic men of the time founded the Board of Trade on July 16, 1895. Its mission was to actively seek out businesses to relocate in Framingham."[6]

Hickory Wheel Company.

48

A PLUM IS PLUCKED

What timing! The Dennison Manufacturing Company was outgrowing its plant in Roxbury and was in the process of looking for a larger facility. The newly formed Board of Trade pounced on this ripe opportunity. Once all the logistics were worked out, an agreement was made for the Para factory to be sold to Dennison for $70,000 and the Board of Trade offered the Company $15,000 to seal the deal. On March 26, 1896, South Framingham became the Dennison Manufacturing Company's new home. With an additional $160,000, Dennison realigned the factory for the production of its products. A gradual change from Roxbury to Framingham took place over the next two years.

Superintendent of Department 3, John Collins, clearly explained the rationale for the move to Framingham in this 1927 interview:

"If the company stayed in Roxbury, the plant would have had to be considerably expanded. Taxes were high there, and the factory was some little distance from the railroad, so that everything had to be trucked. C.S. Dennison wanted to keep the plant with[in] Massachusetts. There was also a feeling that production should be centralized. At Framingham, railroad connections were excellent, taxes were low, and there seemed to be room enough for centralization and indefinite expansion."[7]

From its early settlement, Framingham had a history of welcoming new enterprises. Dennison was no exception; it was embraced with open arms. Historian, Stephen Herring credited the Board of Trade for "arranging one of the greatest marriages between a company and a town in American industrial history."[8]

At the time of the Company's transition to Framingham, Henry Dyer was the president. The most senior family member was Treasurer, Charles S. Dennison, the younger son of E.W. Dennison.[9] Shortly after graduation from Harvard in 1899, Henry S. Dennison, the son of Henry B. Dennison became part of the Dennison Manufacturing Company. Henry, like his grandfather in the 19th century, would become the Company *leader and builder* of the 20th century.

SOUTH FRAMINGHAM

(If not the Hub of the Universe) the Hub of a Territory containing 2,000,000 people within a radius of thirty miles

The Boston & Albany and Old Colony lines diverged in six directions. By 1890, the South Framingham Station welcomed one hundred trains daily.

Centralization

Centering the Dennison Manufacturing Company in Framingham at the turn of the 20th century came at a promising time. The country had finally recovered from the 1893 Depression. General prosperity filled the air! Dennison, like other American companies, was to share in this time of accelerated economic growth. According to E.P. Hayes in *History of the Dennison Manufacturing Company,* 1929, the Company was like a "released spring," in that the "business literally leaped upward" during the early years of the new century.[1] Sales volume reached $1,689.000 in 1897. By 1906, a growth of 163 percent was achieved as sales climbed to $4,451,000.[2] Several factors were credited for this remarkable leap: a new efficient facility, extensive advertising, increase of crepe paper sales and the continual addition of quality merchandise. As a result, the Dennison name attained greater influence, strength and durability as a leader in its field.

During its formative years, Dennison's main emphasis was dominated by the marketing of merchandise. Company decisions were generally made by the sales organization. Now with a booming business centered in Framingham and a heightened demand for products, there was a need to improve and enhance manufacturing. Focus turned to the factory. The need to expand production in order to meet ever-growing demand brought the factory point of view to the forefront. The recent surge in business revealed the need to modernize machinery. At the same time, it was apparent that it was necessary to alter policies that affected factory management. Trust, understanding and cooperation between the two branches were crucial for the good of the whole organization. Closing the *gap* between marketing and manufacturing became the order of the day.

South Framingham factory.
Courtesy of Susan Silva.

Two champions arose to support the importance of strengthening the factory: E.W.'s younger son, Charles S. Dennison and his grandson, Henry S. Dennison. Charles and Henry were first employed by the Company as factory workers. Charles began his work in the machine shop at the Roxbury plant in 1878. In 1899, Henry was hired to work in the wax department. Each of these men learned the ins and outs of factory operations on a first hand basis and understood the need for change. Now, these two like-minded men joined forces to bring about the balance of production and marketing at the Framingham plant. The longed for centralization was on the horizon!

Henry S. Dennison.

Charles S. Dennison, *New York Salesman,* circa 1880. Tintype photograph.

Charles was 20 years old when he began work at the Roxbury factory. He was transferred to New York in 1880 as a salesman to broaden his knowledge of the business. With some factory and selling experience, he was sent to England in 1884 to oversee the London branch and to test the British market. Charles had success in setting up a small wholesale store for stationers in the first year. But, he found at this time, the British market wanted cheaper goods than Dennison had to offer. Charles returned home when his father died in 1886. In 1892 he became a Director. He was elected president in 1909 and held this position until his death in 1912. Charles was a member of the Boston Chamber of Commerce. He served as a director of the Newton Hospital and was appointed to Governor Foss' Massachusetts Employees Insurance Association. A tribute from the August, 1912 *Boston Evening Transcript* reprinted in *Round Robin,* described Charles Dennison as a friendly and democratic man — an exceptional man:

"... his personal friendliness with everyone from office boy to directorate; his quiet efforts to enable his men to do their work at peace with themselves — the first condition of all good work — stamp the exceptional man. His company has that rarity in business life, the family tone."

Next page: Sanborn maps, November 1897 and April 1903.
Sanborn Map Company, New York.

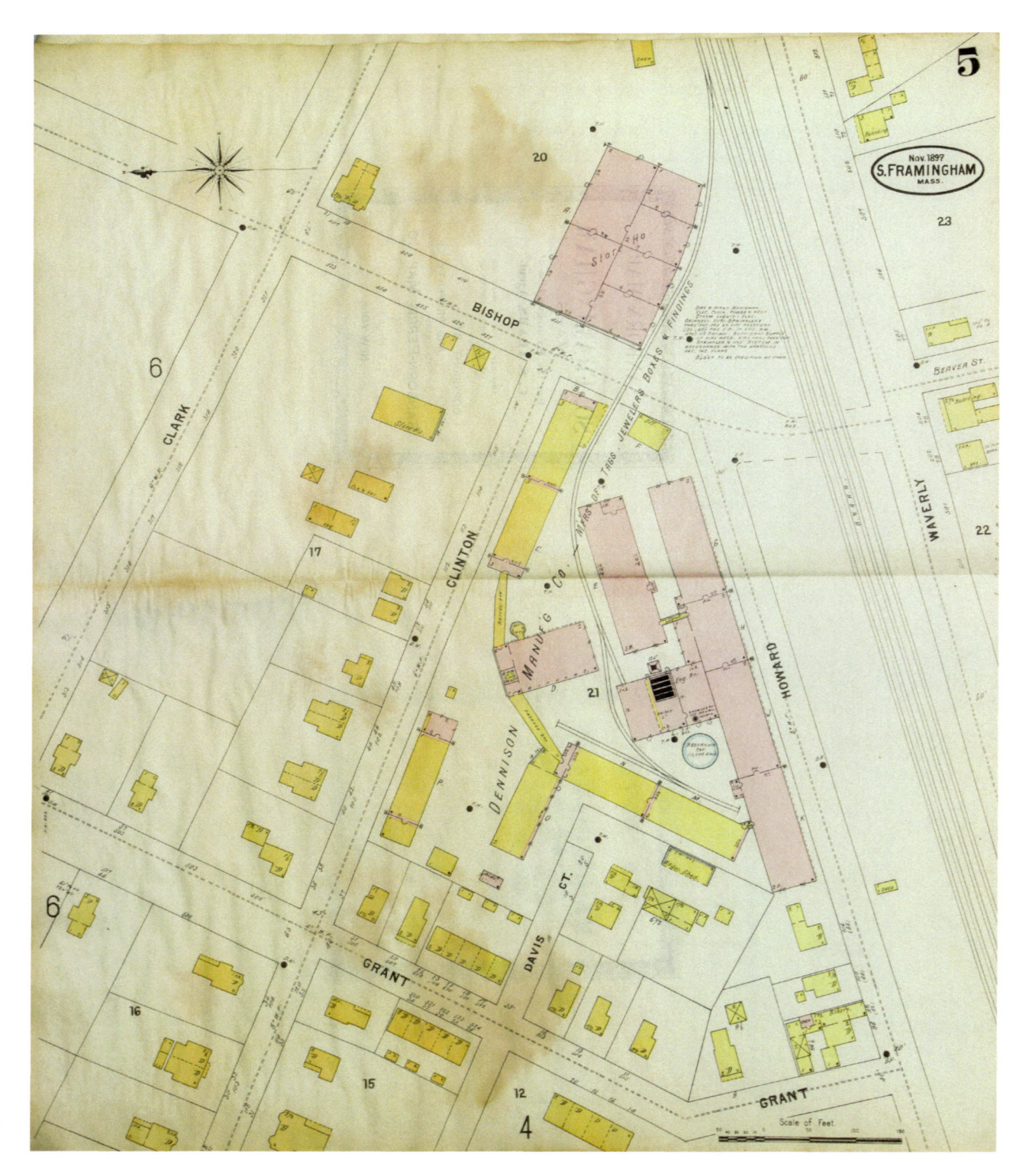

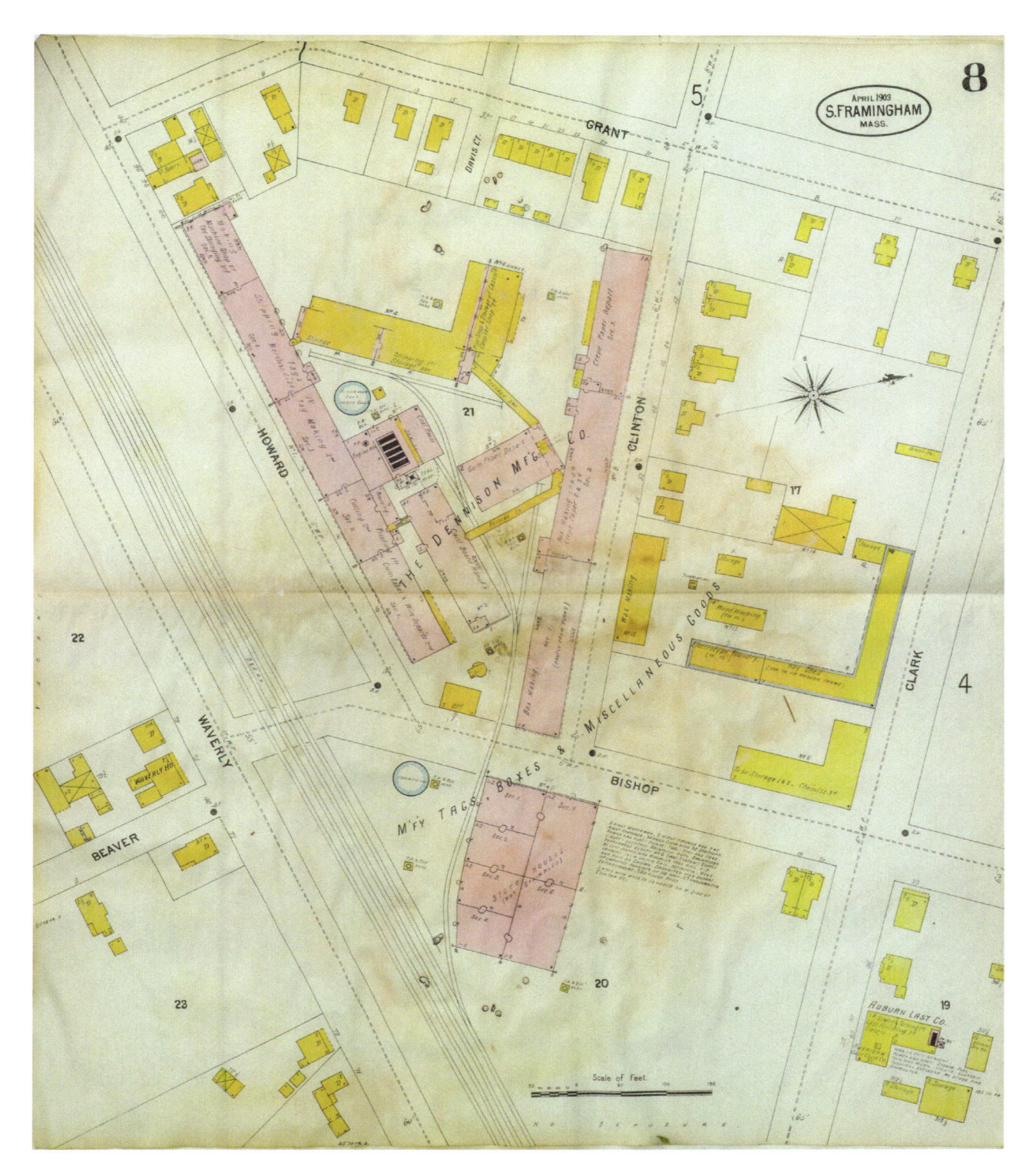

8

APRIL 1903
S. FRAMINGHAM
MASS.

GRANT

DAVIS CT.

5

THE DENNISON MFG CO.

HOWARD

CLINTON

21

17

22

WAVERLY

WAVERLY HO.

BEAVER

M'FY TAGS BOXES & MISCELLANEOUS GOODS

BISHOP

CLARK

4

23

20

19

AUBURN LAST CO.

Scale of Feet

A View of the South Framingham Factory Circa 1904

Stringing marking tags.

Gummed paper sheet cutting.

Paper box and inspection department.

Gummed label cutting.

The Machine Shop.

The Power House.

During the first decade in the new plant, Charles and his nephew, Henry initiated changes in the basic structure of the Company. Improvements began with the development and purchase of new machinery and equipment. From 1897 to 1906, the investment in machinery increased by more than 300%. This was accompanied by the updating of policies. More authority and power to make decisions was given to Frank Pope, the factory superintendent. Under his guidance, management quickly took on the responsibility of upgrading production and efficiency. Salary improvements were made for those who worked in the factory. To keep pace with these advances, the sales force was increased; "Sample" offices were established in key cities; merchandising committees were formed; and product lines were expanded.

The factory and the sales branches scheduled joint meetings to better understand and solve their common problems. The dynamic changes accomplished by the group stimulated all employees and offered them more opportunity for individual development and advancement. Diligence, cooperation and the hard work of management and employees, gradually led to the centralization of marketing and manufacturing in Framingham.

The first salesmen's class, Framingham 1899.

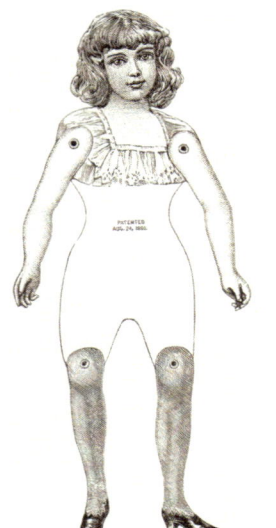

Accessory in Crepe Paper Work.
A new style – Jointed-Doll, 1898 catalogue.

DENNISON'S
"Standard Embossed" Crêpe Paper.

A new idea in crepe paper. The latest line of embossed or raised effects on "Standard" crepe paper for decorative purposes.

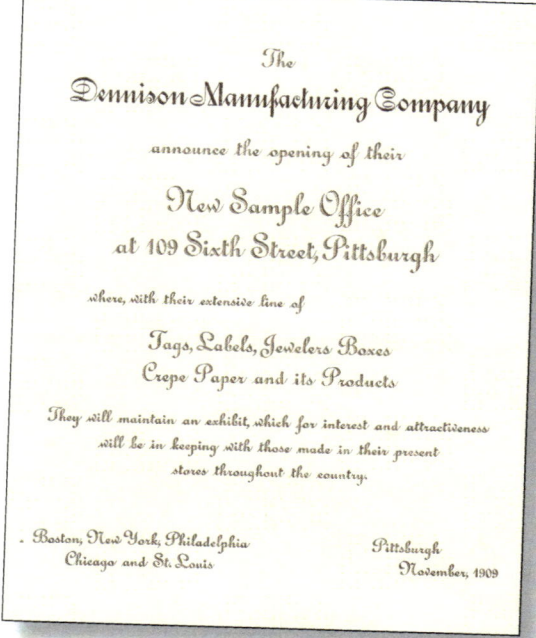

The
Dennison Manufacturing Company
announce the opening of their
New Sample Office
at 109 Sixth Street, Pittsburgh
where, with their extensive line of
Tags, Labels, Jewelers Boxes
Crepe Paper and its Products
They will maintain an exhibit, which for interest and attractiveness
will be in keeping with those made in their present
stores throughout the country.

Boston, New York, Philadelphia
Chicago and St. Louis

Pittsburgh
November, 1909

Sample office announcement.

Policies and Practices

Although Charles and Henry Dennison were shown to be a formidable team, it was Henry who was the key player in the reorganization of the Company's structure. His managerial decisions, ideas, and plans showed that he was Dennison's 20th century *leader and builder* — his grandfather, Eliphalet's counterpart.

A time study was used to determine the most efficient method of completing a task. The picture shows a time study being taken in the Box Division – Department 8A. Miss Katherine Krebs, centre, is taking the time of each operation as performed by Miss Esther Kenigsberg at the right.
– Round Robin, October 1921.

Henry was interested in the scientific approach to business management developed by mechanical engineer, Frederick W. Taylor.[1] According to Taylor's plan: management should determine the best way to do a task; provide the tools and training; and offer incentives for good work. Tasks should be broken down into small parts, analyzed and timed. Taylor suggested that adherence to this methodical approach would increase worker productivity. The influence of Taylor's principles, coupled with Dennison's growing emphasis on human relations, influenced the development of many innovative programs.

Among Henry's early programs, three plans brought him extensive acclaim throughout the business world. An abbreviated explanation of these policies, taken primarily from *The Dennison Manufacturing Co.,* 1922 follows: (1) Managerial Industrial Partnership Plan (2) Employee Industrial Partnership Plan (3) The Unemployment Fund.

MANAGERIAL INDUSTRIAL PARTNERSHIP PLAN

In 1878, when the Company was incorporated, all stock was held by the managers, or what Henry's grandfather called the "principal helpers." These men, who held common stock, had total control of the business and shared in all its profits. Over time, due to death and resignation, the stock passed to individuals outside the Company. Many of the outsiders had no connection to the business and had no idea of Dennison's current concerns. But, they held the power to vote for

Industrial Partnership certificate held by Charles S. Dennison for twenty-five shares, May 13, 1912.

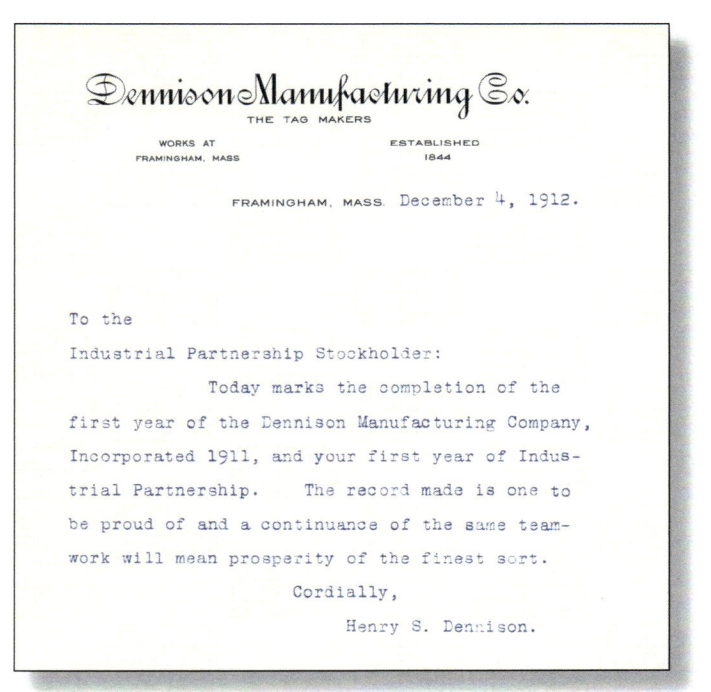

Letter from H.S. Dennison to the Industrial Partnership stockholders praising the success of the Partnerships' first year, December 4, 1912.

the Directors. In order to maintain the Company's interests, Henry believed it was crucial to return voting control to the management, to those who held the most influence. With this in mind, he and Charles restructured the business in 1911. At the time of the reorganization, The Managerial Industrial Partnership Plan was devised. Under this Plan, only managerial personnel could hold stock with the right to vote for the Directors. Managers were entitled to an annual cash dividend. The stock also became non-transferable. Control was now successfully placed back into the hands of those who actively participated in the management of the Company.

EMPLOYEE INDUSTRIAL PARTNERSHIP PLAN
Employee Co-Operative Plan and Works Committee

Henry believed business policies would be strengthened if those employees who were in non-managerial positions could make recommendations to management that related to their own work. He encouraged workers to design a proposal for this purpose. In 1919, an elected committee of employees drafted the Employees Co-Operative Plan. Under the plan, a Works Committee was formed in October. This elected committee of fifty-four members had one representative from each department of the factory. The group met regularly to discuss departmental issues and then submitted their suggestions to management.[2] Implementation of the Committee's many useful recommendations led to increased productivity and greater profits. As a result of their numerous contributions, the employees thought they had earned the right to share in the Company profits. Management agreed! The following year, the Employee Industrial Partnership Plan[3] was devised by the Works Committee. It was similar in structure to that of the managerial group. The

The first Works Committee, December 1919.

workers received non-transferable Employee Stock, which entitled them to the same rate of cash dividend as management. However, unlike management, they had no voting rights. It was felt that the employees already shared in management of the business through the voice of the Works Committee. The completion of this plan made Dennison "a true industrial partner." On January 1, 1921, 1,696 employees became part of the Employee Industrial Partnership Plan.[4]

To offer a better understanding of factory operations and to strengthen their commitment, management invited new Employee Industrial Partners to tour the Framingham factory. The Worcester Group. – *Round Robin,* April 1922.

Distributing the E.I.P. certificates and cash. On the left is A.D. McDonald of Dept. 7A, receiving the check. In the center is H.C. Buzzell, Works Committee representative, and on the right, W.F. Wentworth, Division Manager. – *Round Robin,* April 1926.

THE UNEMPLOYMENT FUND

In 1916, Henry Dennison laid the foundation for the *first* private Unemployment Fund in the United States. This program gave workers job protection, financial relief and it helped to curtail the rate of worker turnover. Company Directors set aside a sum of money each year to support and grow the fund, which totaled $150,000 by 1921.[5]

The Works Committee was asked to develop guidelines for distributing the fund to the unemployed. The following terms were set in place: Before an employee was laid off, every effort was to be made by management to find a suitable position through a transfer. If a transfer was not possible, and the worker was laid off for a half day or more in a week and had dependents, he/she received 80% of their wages. A worker without dependents received 60% of his/her pay. The Plan not only offered security, but it also encouraged employees to remain interested in the success of the Company.

The August, 1927 issue of *Round Robin* featured an interesting request from the Company to its employees. The appeal came as a result of high demand on the Unemployment Fund in1926, which continued into the summer of 1927.

BOARD OF DIRECTORS (1920)
CHARLES E. BENSON   JOHN P. WILLS   WILLIAM E. P. HOWELL   THOMAS G. PORTMORE
HORACE LOCKWOOD   HENRY S. DENNISON   HAROLD B. HAYDEN

Board of Directors, 1920.

> **ORIGINAL RULES FOR UNEMPLOYMENT BENEFITS:**
>
> *"After paying benefits for six consecutive days, the committee shall consider whether the condition of the fund permits continuation of payments and if so, at what rate."* – Round Robin, March 1920, 10.
>
> **Employees taking a temporary job outside of the Company at a lower wage would be compensated for the difference. If a worker was transferred within the Company to a lower wage position, the difference would be added.**

In order to avoid temporary transfers and unemployment, workers were asked to suggest "unemployment items" as "fill-in" goods to be manufactured when regular work in a department was slow. As an example, the article suggested the miniature crepe paper party or "monkey" cap, which had been introduced for this purpose in early 1927. Women in the Crepe Paper Department made these little hats as a "fill in" product during this slack period. With

The addition of greeting cards helped to maintain an even flow of factory work throughout the year. This design was featured in 1921.

MERRY CHRISTMAS   AND HAPPY NEW YEAR

everyone thinking, Dennison believed that its employees would be able to recommend a number of items that could be made during quiet times. The article also reminded employees that "accepted suggestions which have definite money value to the company, will as always, be considered for special awards." *(See suggestion system on page 62.)*

James Armington, Chairman of the crepe committee, demonstrates one of the latest creations, "The Monkey Cap."

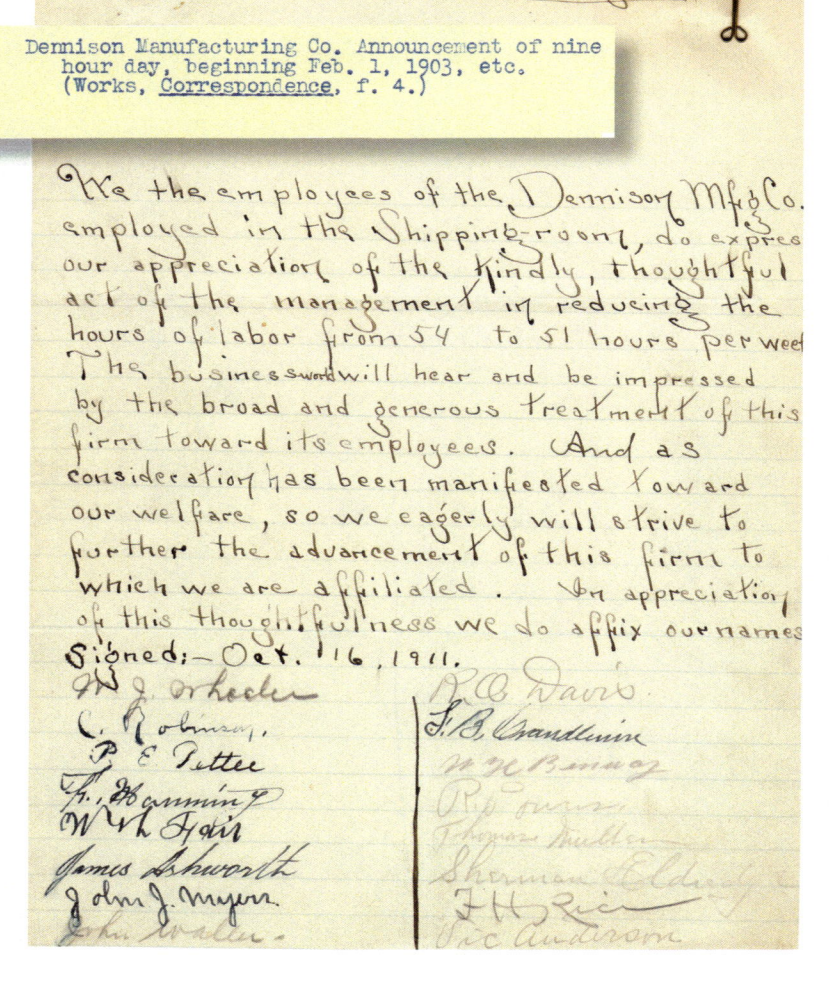

Office memo announcing the beginning of the fifty-four hour week.

Working Hours

The customary sixty hour work week was limited to fifty-four hours in 1903. It was then reduced to fifty-one hours in 1911. Over time the work week was further reduced to forty-eight hours and finally to today's customary forty hour week.

In 1925, the work day began at 7:45am and ended at 5:30pm with a one hour break for lunch. A warning whistle blew seven minutes before opening time. Two minutes before starting time, a gong rang twice and the gates were closed. Everyone was to be in their respective departments

Sixty-three members of the Shipping Department thank Mr. H.S. Dennison for the reduction of hours in 1911.

and ready for the day's work at the sound of a double gong. At closing time a gong sounded followed by a quick burst of the whistle. And *everyone* scurried out through the open factory gates!

The closing of the day.

The opening of the day.

Employees exit through the Howard Street gate.

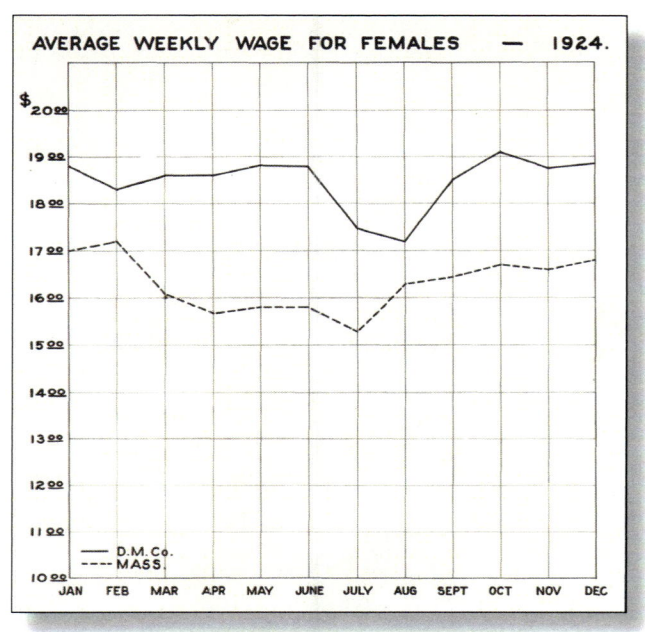

Average weekly wage for females, 1924.

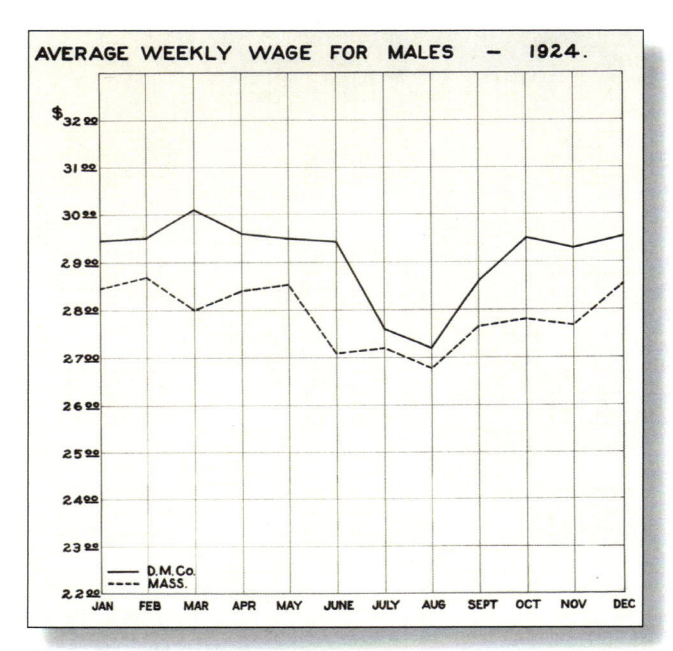

Average weekly wage for males, 1924.

On September 15th, 1923, the third annual outing began with a parade down Concord Street past the Kendall Hotel and the St. George Theatre. – *Round Robin,* September 1923.

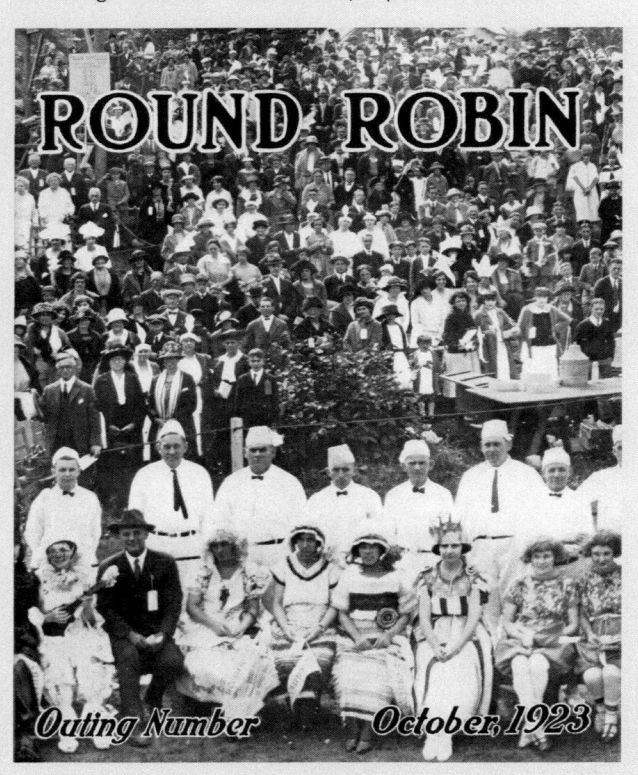

The afternoon outing was held at Norumbega Park in Aburndale, Massachusetts. Seated second from left is Henry S. Dennison, among five thousand employees and their families, enjoying "one continuous round of fun." – *Round Robin,* October 1923.

"People" Programs

Dennison Manufacturing Company was a forerunner in creating programs for the well-being of its employees. The Company thoughtfully founded and tested many diverse plans in the early 1900s. Of particular interest were those "projects which dealt with the human element in industry." As programs were organized, Dennison put the responsibility of their management into the hands of the employees; they took the active role. Management's role was minimal; it was readily available and willing to assist if requested.

Information from *Dennison Institutions,* 1925, and *Some Dennison's Plans and Practices,* 1928, was used to outline the following "projects." In addition, anecdotes of people, places and events were gathered from issues of *Round Robin* and other sources to give a "You Are There" momentary view of these distinctive "People" Programs.

THE SUGGESTION SYSTEM

In 1900, the Suggestions System was instituted. This new program encouraged employees to contribute ideas that would improve the efficiency of the plant's operations. These might include adjustments or additions to machinery, product, safety or packaging.

An employee's suggestion was submitted, recorded, and then sent to one of several committees such as Manufacturing, Holiday or Merchandising for evaluation. If a suggestion was accepted by one of the committees, an appropriate award was issued. Employees generally received a cash award of $5 for their first idea and a certificate signed by the

A suggestion committee in session.
Left to right, A.L. Paulsen, W.F. McNally,
W.E. Maloney, H.F. Scott, and L.W. Leach.

Miss Doris Dalrymple
handles receiving,
forwarding, and filing of
suggestions.

A.L. Paulsen, left, watches as
John Day explains his suggestion, with
Miss Evelyn Gleason seated at the machine.

Company president and treasurer. A framed picture of the Framingham Plant or the Brunswick, Maine Plant was awarded for an employee's second suggestion. Twenty-five dollars was given to those who had submitted ten winning recommendations.

To inspire potential "suggestors," the Company introduced specialty prizes. In March of 1916, a tempting specialty was added. A choice of $30 or three shares of Dennison Second Preferred Stock was offered to employees who had ten accepted suggestions.

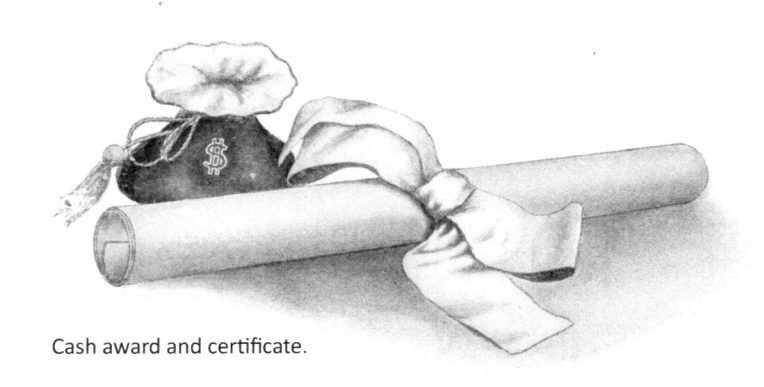

Cash award and certificate.

In 1926, "Suggestor" E.V. Christensen of Department 22 received a check for $500.

Over the years cash prizes varied from $3 to $100 and occasionally the dollar amount soared much higher. In 1926, E.V. Christensen of Department 22, Mechanical Planning and Drafting, received a $500 check for what the Company considered an invaluable idea that dealt with controlling waste. This was indeed an impressive sum!

In 1900, 267 suggestions were submitted and twenty-six of these were accepted. As interest grew, more and more ideas flowed into the suggestion box. The year 1923 brought 4,128 entries with 1,156 awards. A total of $3,319 in cash was distributed, as well as many certificates and framed pictures. This was a banner year!

An employee making a suggestion, 1904.

The following are examples of winning suggestions that were put into practice:

1. One or more days would be set aside as Children's Day when a product demonstration was to be held in a department store.

2. Lights were to be installed on all crepe machines.

3. Wedding Ring Folders made of the Mother of Pearl Paper, was suggested by Mr. William Hillard, winner of a $25 cash prize in 1925.

4. Ring and cuff link boxes with a base elegantly covered in satin or velvet brought Margaret Gormley a $50 award.

Many workers received multiple awards. R.J. Brown of Department 30W, the Warehouse Division, held top honors with 90 suggestions by 1927! And finally, Miss Genevieve Shanley received her second $10 award for submitting a new Halloween invitation in 1928. Her bewitching design was launched in the 1929 Halloween Line. Over the years, thoughtful solutions touched every facet of Dennison's business operations, which resulted in better working conditions for all employees.

"The Kiddies' Corner in our Chicago Store where the little tots are taught how to make all sorts of things from Dennison products." – Round Robin, March 1921.

Dennison took an interest in children's crafts. In 1910, most of the Company stores had a program called "A Children's Playhouse." Children were invited to take part in a class where young ladies taught them how to make crafts using Dennison products. They might make kites, soldier caps, dolls and doll outfits, or perhaps a colorful whirling pinwheel.

R.J. Brown.

Perhaps this was a result of suggestion #95, March 1900. *(Photo, 1904)*

#95. *Will you please consider my suggestion of putting a covering over the bicycle rack. Of course, we are most grateful for the rack, but at present the wheels remain in the sun all day, and on stormy days we are obliged to go down four flights of stairs to carry them in. I believe if necessary the cyclists would be willing to contribute toward the expenses.*

#71. *I have an idea of a small machine for cutting twine instead of the way we cut it at present. I am pretty sure we can make it work. It will do away with a lot of old traps, besides saving a lot of time. I cannot tell you what it is like very well here, but if you wish to, I will tell it to whoever you wish me to.*

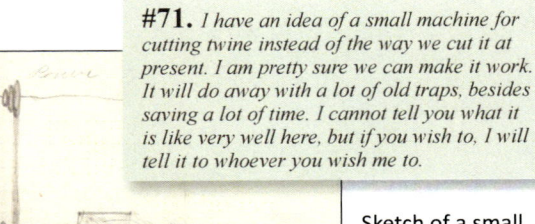

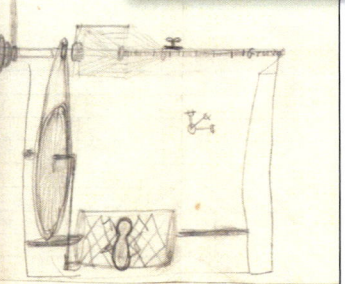

Sketch of a small machine for cutting twine, March 17, 1900.

FINANCIAL PROGRAMS

The Dennison Manufacturing Company Credit Union was incorporated on January 26, 1917 as a savings and loan association. Members of the Credit Union could save money and obtain loans at a reasonable rate.

As early as 1905, the Company offered a Savings Fund. Employees made a weekly payment, which was deposited in a local bank. The bank would then distribute the earnings twice a year — June and December — just in time for summer vacation and Christmas expenses.

"Late in 1916 the D. M. C. Credit Union was formed in a 'cooperative' spirit 'to promote thrift among its members by giving them an opportunity to save money in small amounts and to obtain loans at moderate rates for purposes which promise to be of benefit to the borrower.'"
– Industrial Relations: 1920-1929, 137.

Dennison Savings and Loans – So many possibilities!
Round Robin cartoon, 1925.

The Payroll Department handled the funds.

Left: Collecting for the Christmas Fund. Left to right, Miss Bernice Powers and Miss Nora O'Hare. – *Round Robin,* 1925.

Right: Laden with Christmas Bundles. Left to right, Misses Katherine Kellett, Elizabeth McIntyre, Lena Mutti, and Ruth Hagar. – *Round Robin,* January 1925.

Correspondents Department goes to the beach.

"Jim" Cunningham and his daughter Mary.

A notable fund, the Framingham Building and Loan Fund, was established in 1920. Its purpose was to encourage individual home ownership and to offer loans for second mortgages. If an employee wished to build or purchase a home and was in need of a second mortgage, this fund offered a loan at a reasonable rate. A sum of $100,000 was initially set aside for this Housing Fund, which was placed in the hands of three trustees for distribution.

A new house!

Central Library / Traveling Bookcase

When the library was first opened, it contained technical and industrial books that appealed primarily to business specialists. However, it wasn't long before additional subjects were added to attract everyone in the factory. Biographies, poetry, current events, magazines, fiction, non-fiction and pamphlets were found among the publications which soon filled the shelves. An experienced librarian was available to assist the workers in their search for subjects and materials. The library's uncomplicated system allowed an employee to easily borrow books for a two week period. Leaving his/her name and department number was all that was required.

F.A. Mooney, Librarian, on the step ladder getting a book for a visitor. – *Round Robin,* 1925.

"The Library" page offered reading suggestions for your vacation. Perhaps *A Passage to India* or *The Sea and the Jungle?*

Your Library Offers You

INFORMATION on any subject

BOOKS to be read at home for pleasure, instruction and profit

TELEPHONE SERVICE for answering difficult questions

Do you have a difficult question?

Education is a life-long process.

Dennison promoted the use of its library services in a variety of ways. In order to encourage everyone to take advantage of its resources, an informative bi-monthly publication called *The Library Review* was available. In the mid-1920s, issues of *Round Robin* included a page called "The Library." This page highlighted and suggested books, topics and activities that might be of interest to employees. On one occasion, it reminded readers that the Library offered telephone service, which was available to answer any *difficult* question. The Library page was first to introduce employees to an innovative American Library Association program called *Read with a Purpose.* Using the program guidelines, the librarian organized a variety of subjects with appropriate materials into reading courses. Health, Great American Books, Economics and Psychology were among the first topics that were offered. Psychology was found to be one of the most popular courses of study. The librarian also set up individual reading courses upon request.

An exceptional service offered by the library was the Traveling Bookcase. Fiction and non-fiction books were made available to employees on a regular schedule through two Libraries-on-Wheels. Each of the thirty-six departments had a bookcase visit accompanied by a librarian at least once a month. Dennison purchased some of the books, but most were borrowed from the Framingham Public Library. Perhaps *Kim* by Rudyard Kipling, *From Earth to Moon* by Jules Verne or Catherine Filene's, *Careers for Women* might be among the choices brought by the cart on its most recent round. Titles were routinely added and exchanged. Monthly issues of *Round Robin* listed the new selections and sometimes a lively sketch of an available book was featured. Employees were encouraged to send a request to the library if there was a particular title that they would like to borrow. As many as 300 volumes, new titles and old, journeyed on each set of wheels throughout the plant — right into the readers' hands. In 1921, nearly 7,000 books circulated throughout the factory aboard the traveling bookcases.

In 1926, Dennison made a unique arrangement with Bates and Holdsworth, a Framingham stationery store. Bates and Holdsworth agreed to place popular fiction in

Traveling bookcase.

Traveling bookcase advance notice sign.

Readers were thinkers!

the Dennison Library and also on the shelves of the Lunch Room. Books like *Show Boat* and *The Silver Spoons* were now available shortly after publication. Employees conveniently borrowed these up-to-date books for three cents a day from the new Circulating Library. What a novel idea!

It appears that Dennison felt that its Library was indispensable — whatever anyone needed was to be found in a book. Readers were thinkers! And the educated reader contributed to a strong workforce.[1]

SAMPLE / DISPLAY ROOM

This room featured a myriad of Dennison products that employees could purchase. A salesman assisted shoppers with their purchases on Monday, Wednesday and Friday during the noon lunch break. The purchased items were then available for pick up at the Grant or Howard Street gate on Tuesday and Thursday at 5:30pm or at noontime on Saturday.

The Sample/Display Room, full of artistically arranged items was a very attractive drawing card, especially during the holiday seasons. October brought out jet black cats, sleepy bats, and a cunning witch on a broomstick, adrift in the midnight sky. Not to be missed in October of 1926, was the swashbuckling pirate, Captain Kidd.

A commanding figure was he; garbed in his dashing crepe paper costume with fearsome saber tightly clutched by his side. A glowing Christmas tree decorated with fanciful crepe paper

A view of one end of the new Sample/Display Room at the factory, 1916.

Cartoon drawn by a member of the salesmen's class, March 1916.

Captain Kidd, 1926.

Glowing Christmas tree decorated with fanciful crepe paper, 1926.

Seventy enthusiastic girls enjoyed an evening craft class in the Sample/Display Room conducted by Miss Lang and Miss Marshall, May 31, 1923.

whimsies took center stage in December. There were craft kits, party caps, streamers and stars … valentines, shamrocks and abundant reminders of spring — what a Buyers Paradise!

A visit to the Sample/Display Room not only offered an opportunity to purchase merchandise, but it also gave workers a chance to see what was made in different factory departments. It was a perfect way to keep up with the Company's most recent products. The employees received a discount of 20% on purchases in 1925, which was raised to 35% in 1928.

Confetti, flyers and serpentines – pleasant reminders of spring.

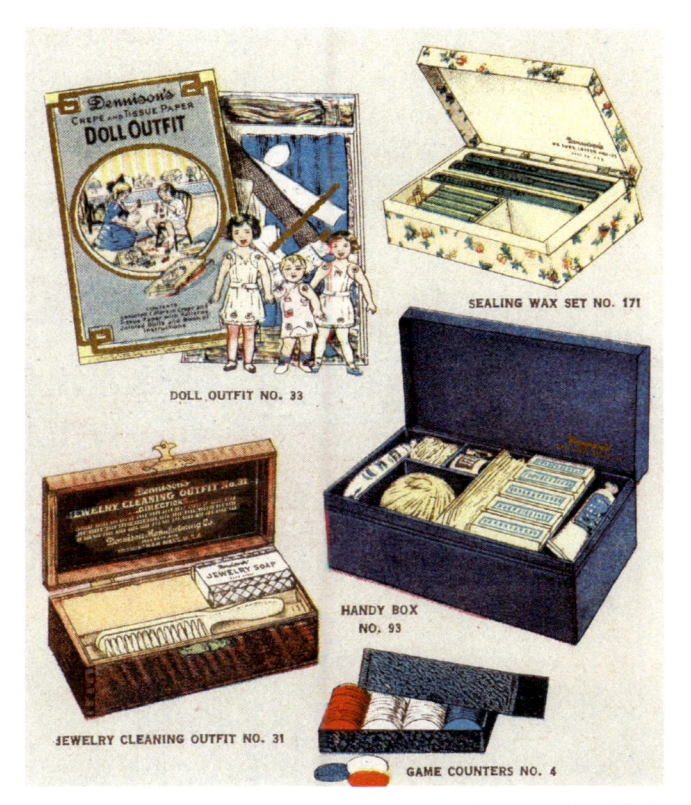

Product samples, 1920.

Price list document, 1880.

HISTORY ROOM

In 1920, Henry Dennison hired the Company's first historian, T.P. Martin. The historian was responsible for systematizing the Company's past history and compiling information on current trends. Scrapbooks, catalogues, product samples, photographs, reports, and documents of all types were among the thousands of items that were placed into the archives. Mr. Martin also served as a research librarian, locating and organizing specific materials upon request.

In order to house and share the growing collection, the History Room was opened on May 25, 1922. This impressive new fireproof room was a safe haven for the preservation of the developing archives. It included a space for research and study, and cabinets to showcase the old and the new. It offered a pleasant, inviting atmosphere.

Dennison's Handy Boxes catalogue cover, 1911.

A new History Room, 1922.

The historian organized exhibitions using samples from the archives and items given or loaned to the Company by generous contributors. Crepe paper lamp shades and hats, boxes and tags, or sealing wax novelties might be on display to catch the viewer's eye. Perhaps a visitor would be lucky enough to see the old account book that belonged to E.W. Dennison in 1839 when he was a young man of nineteen. This rare book was a record of his first retail jewelry business in Bath, Maine. One of the entries showed that E.W. bought boxes from his father's Brunswick workshop in the mid-1840s for his shop. Prominently displayed in July of 1922, was a lamp used in the old Brunswick factory during the Civil War Era. This was kindly donated by the Misses Ellen and Olive Chase. Another treasure was a 1768 letter written by David Dennison, grandfather of shoemaker Andrew Dennison. His cordial letter asks his brother Isaac to send a barrel of turpentine to coat a boat's deck and some turnip seed. David's letter and a transcription were presented in the September, 1927 issue of *Round Robin* accompanied by this playful comment: "He would not last long in a spelling bee!"

History Room wax exhibit, May 1924.

Innovative crepe paper lamp shade, 1911.

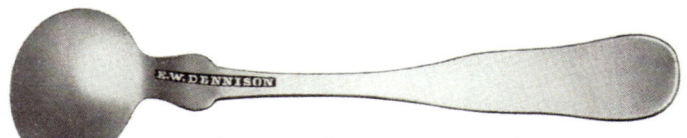

1846 silver spoon from E.W. Dennison's Bangor, Maine jewelry shop. On display in the History Room in December of 1926.

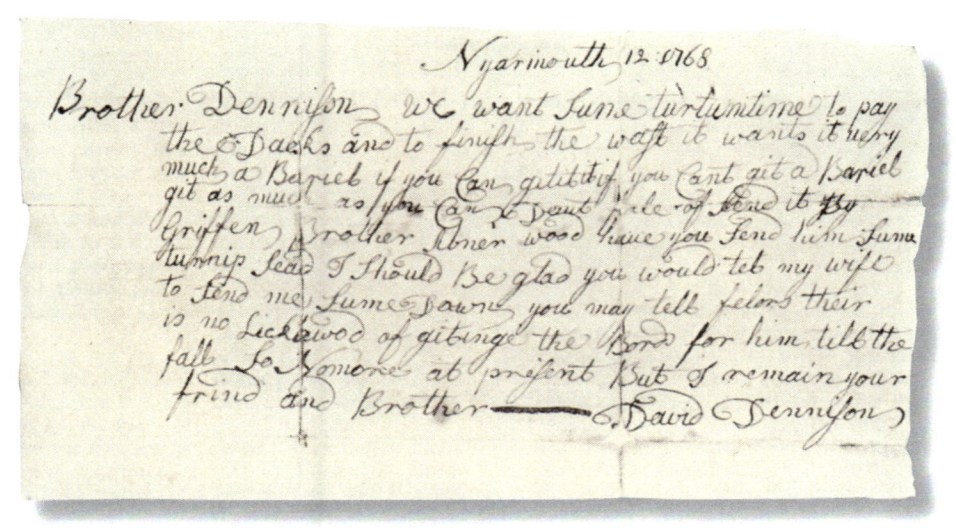

Letter written by David Dennison to his brother Isaac, 1768.

1856 Dennison ring box on display in the History Room in October of 1926.

On May 5, 1924, the History Room opened a special exhibit of boxes and cases. Early ring cases from 1844 were displayed next to those that were shown at the 1893 Chicago World's Fair. The most up-to-date boxes complemented these "oldsters" of the past.

The opening of this exhibit was of particular interest because Dennison welcomed its suppliers and customers to display their own products. Firms that provided materials for box production and those that used the Company's finished products responded. The construction of boxboard was presented by The New Haven Pulp & Board Company, and F.W. Rauskolb Company described the steps needed to make gold leaf for decoration. The Waltham Watch Company displayed watch parts as well as finished watches set in Dennison cases. Conklin Pen Manufacturing Company showed pens and pencils snugly nestled in Dennison boxes. Elizabeth Arden and Marshall Field & Company were also among the exhibitors.

The files of the collection not only accurately recorded the Company's

Special exhibit of old boxes and cases, May 1924.

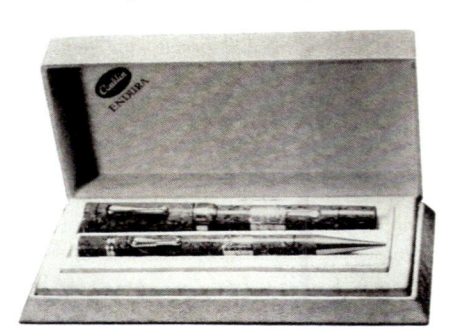

Conklin pen and pencil contained in a Dennison case, 1924.

Dawne Buckley discovers valuable treasures of the company's past from the History Room files. Dennison's Bishop Street warehouse, September 18, 2012.
Courtesy Dana Ricciardi.

development, but the documentation found within, was carefully analyzed. Esther Staples, Dennison historian, emphasized the importance of the files in her 1930 article, "A History Room That Pays Its Way:"

> *"These files hold the most valuable treasure of the company's History Room."* They provide, *"the wanted facts from the past to help the company's executives better meet the problems of the present."*[2]

New problems are not always as new as they appear!

MEN'S MUTUAL RELIEF ASSOCIATION / WOMEN'S MUTUAL RELIEF ASSOCIATION

Employees were insured under the Massachusetts Workman's Compensation Law of 1912, which covered injuries received on the job. In addition, Dennison's Men's and Women's Mutual Relief Associations offered their members monetary help in times of sickness or disability. The two self-supporting organizations charged a monthly membership fee of 25 cents for women and 40 cents for men. Under these plans, a disabled or ill member was offered a fixed monetary benefit each week for a determined period of time. A death benefit of $75 for men and $50 for women was included. Arrangements were made in 1922 for Associates to purchase a Hospital Insurance Plan for $2 each year. Under this plan, a member received hospital care for a rate of $3 per day, which covered twenty-one days each year.

Each organization contributed additional money from their Special Fund to members and charitable groups, individuals and the community. The Women's Association made a donation to the Red Cross and War Relief work in 1919. A check for $25 was presented by the Men's Association to a member who had been out of work for a year due to an accident.

In 1919-1921, the two groups organized a mixed chorus under the direction of Herbert Wellington Smith, a prominent Boston and New York baritone. The chorus offered public concerts for two seasons under Mr. Smith's direction. From this group, several voices emerged to sing with the newly formed Men's Glee Club.[3]

Men's and Women's Mutual Relief Associations gave a concert to an audience of 500 in the Grace Church.

Salt and Pepper

TWO DANCES

APRIL
18th

MAY
3rd

IT'S to be at the Casino in Framingham on Wednesday, May 3rd—a May Party and Dance, under the joint auspices of the Women's and Men's Mutual Relief Associations.

Dance announcement, 1922. *Round Robin* Cartoon, 1922.

Women's Mutual Relief Association takes Saturday afternoon hike to Framingham's Nobscot Mountain.

The Men's and Women's Mutual Relief Association and the Dennison Associates sponsored the first outing to Norumbega Park. Boarding three special trains at the Framingham station, September 10, 1921.

A variety of social events were held to raise funds by each group as well. There was plenty of fun for 50 cents at the Civic League Halloween Party in 1926. The Casino, a dance hall in downtown Framingham, Waushakum Park in South Framingham and the Casino at Saxonville were attractive crowd pleasers for social gatherings and meetings.

LUNCH ROOM

A small lunch room opened in 1909. By the 1920s a new lunch room served approximately 600 employees each day and provided more than 3,000 meals each week. At this time, dinner could be purchased for 30 cents. Corn muffins were two for 5 cents, stews 10 cents, coffee 5 cents and a fancy French pastry rounded off a meal for 6 cents. Ox Tail or Mock Turtle soup simmered overnight in "steam jacket kettles" made a delicious warm winter lunch.

Behind the factory, Company gardener, Randell Steele, worked busily in the large summer garden. Employees enjoyed tasty meals prepared with freshly grown vegetable throughout the growing season. Before the feel of fall filled the air, the Lunch Room personnel put up as many as 500 jars of tomatoes and 200 quarts of piccalilli from the produce grown in the Dennison garden — that delicious taste of summer for those frosty winter months!

Randell Steele in the Lunch Room Garden behind the factory, 1917.

Dennison preserving labels, 1921 catalogue.

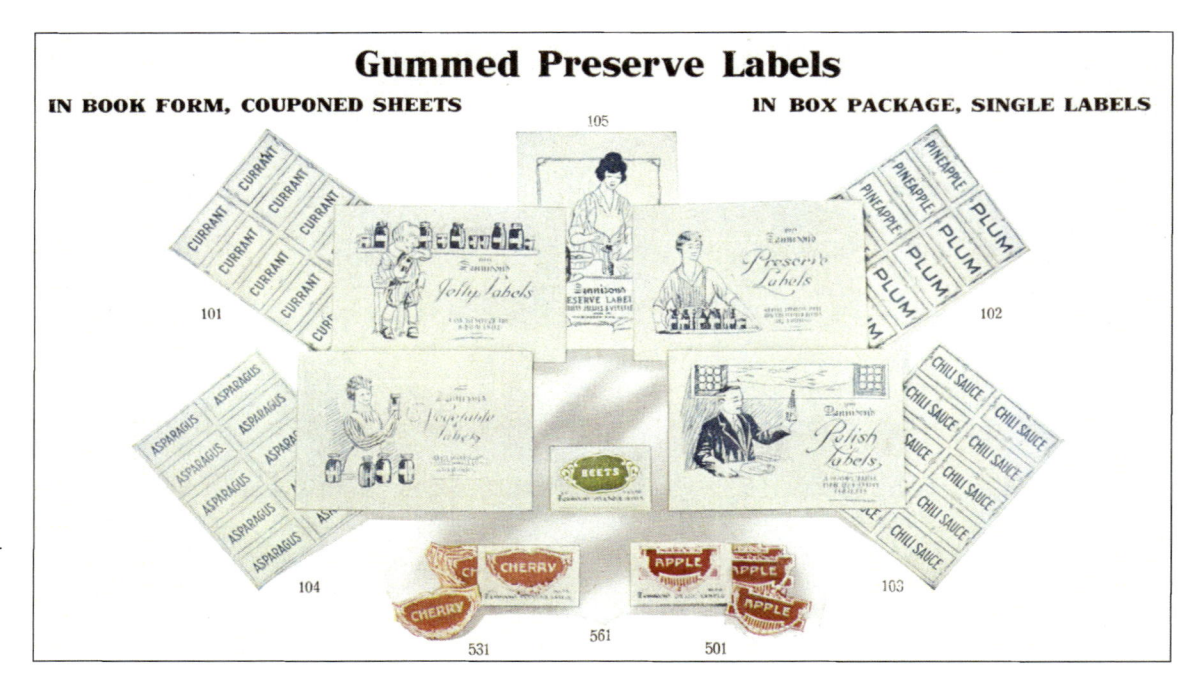

Lunch Room decorated for Thanksgiving dinner, 1920.

THANKSGIVING—WE AGREE

Two attractions – a tasty Thanksgiving dinner with some lively music. *Round Robin* cartoon, 1921.

Each year on Wednesday before Thanksgiving, an old fashioned turkey dinner appeared. A feast for 40 cents included all the basic fixins' topped off with the traditional plum pudding, fruits, cakes and assorted pies. Fanciful holiday decorations and music filled the air, creating a joyous party atmosphere.

When is a lunch room *more* than a lunch room? In 1925, the Fifth Art Exhibit was held in this inviting room. Harvard's Fogg Art Museum graciously loaned ten etchings by noted American artists. The Museum also sent the necessary materials to show the steps taken by an artist to produce his final piece of art. Dennison published an instructive and interesting pamphlet, *How Etchings Are Made* to accompany the exhibit, which was included in the December issue of *Round Robin*.

Curious on-lookers were fascinated by energetic Mexican Jumping Beans that were on display in October of 1926. When warmed up, these petite "hoppers" roll and tumble like accomplished acrobats. Perhaps these amazing little creatures piqued employee interest for the upcoming winter exhibit of Native Arts and Crafts, sent to Mr. Dennison from distant corners of the world.

The fifth art exhibit in the Lunch Room, held in February of 1925.

MEDICAL SERVICES

Dennison was one of the first companies to see the importance of medical care for its employees. The Hospital Department, attended by one nurse, first opened in the spring of 1909 as an experiment. By 1913 it consisted of a reception room, treatment room, a private office and a rest room for women.[4] A part-time physician was hired in 1914. Two years later the Clinic expanded to five rooms. The need was definitely there and medical services quickly began to grow.

Employees could visit the clinic during factory working hours. Minor illnesses and injuries were attended to quickly, which gave employees a sense of security. By 1918, a full time physician, Dr. Murray, and two nurses were available to attend those in need

The Early Treatment Room.

Dr. Halstead Murray, 1922.

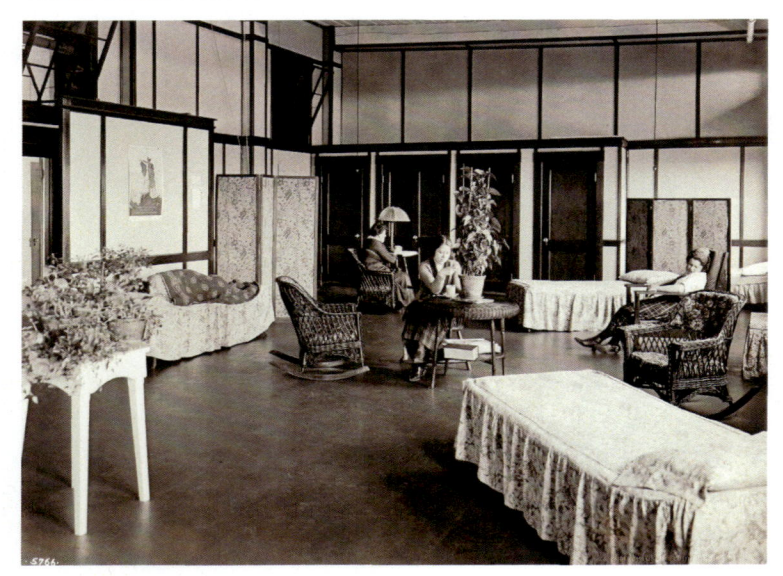

The Ladies Restroom, 1921.

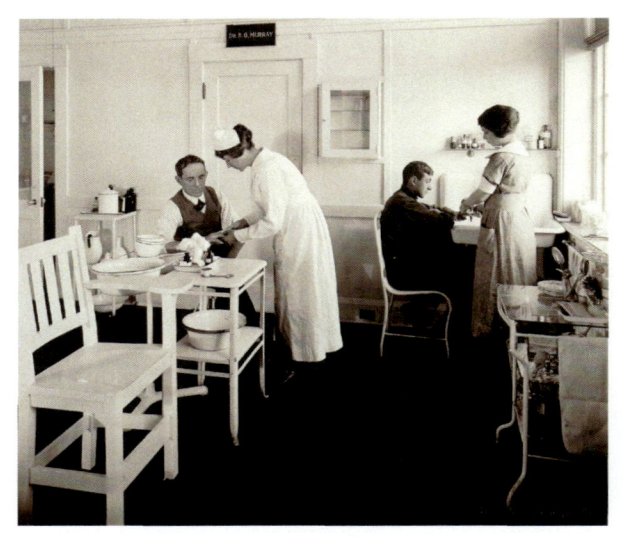

The Clinic Treatment Room, 1922. Left to right, Mr. Mahaney, Miss Fiske, Mr. Paridisi, and Miss Kelley.

at no charge. A Dental Clinic was added in 1922. Workers could consult with Dennison's full time dentist for a free examination or emergency work. A reasonable charge was made for permanent work and dental materials.

In 1914, a diverse group of men interested in ways of improving our Nation's health and prolonging human life, founded an organization known as The Life Extension Institute.[5] Preventive care, rather than waiting for an illness to strike was emphasized by this group. Dr. Eugene Fisk, the group's Director of Hygiene, devised the Periodic Physical Examination, which he saw as a first step in maintaining good health. Influenced by this concept, the Dennison Clinic first offered annual physical examinations to its employees in 1920. Workers were encouraged to visit the Clinic — to seek advice or attention before sickness occurred — to maintain good health. Two years later, *Round Robin* reported that the results of physical exams had proved valuable in correcting those problems which were identified in the early stages. It noted that the majority of employees, who followed the doctor's recommendation, showed marked improvement on their next visit.

Keeping prevention in mind, the clinic informed workers of prevalent health dangers and offered solutions. Nineteen twenty-five brought an

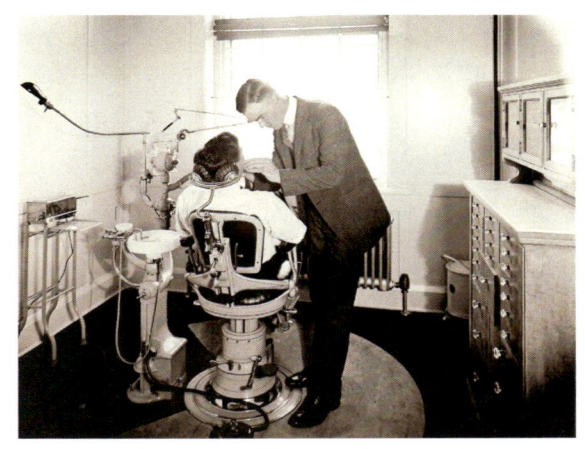

New Dental Clinic, 1922.
Dr. E.C. Stewart examines a patient.

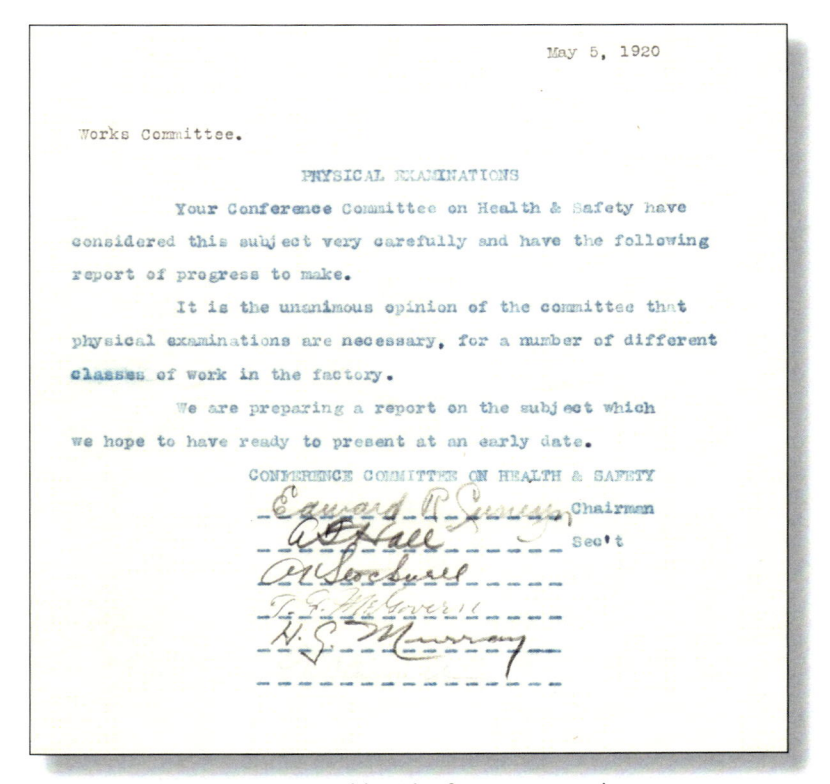

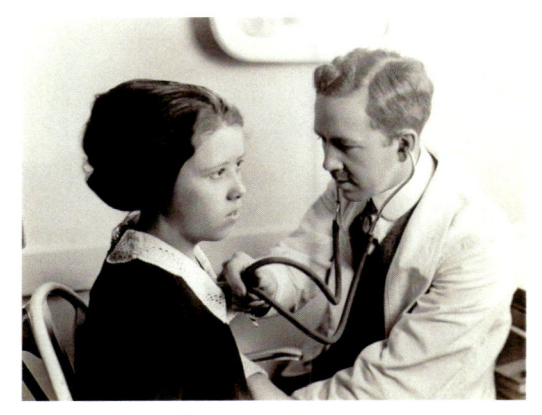

Dr. Murray examines a young woman.

The Dennison Committee on Health and Safety recommends the physical examination for employees. May 5, 1920.

Prevention posters were found on bulletin boards throughout the factory, 1943.

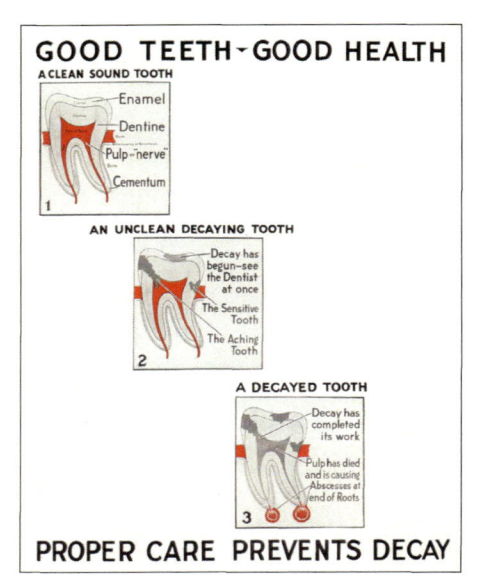

Issues of the *Round Robin* promoted healthy habits, 1924.

PREVENTIVE MEASURE

"An ultra-violet, or sun lamp 'for treatment of certain diseases of the winter months, which can be benefited by sunlight' had been installed." — E.P. Hayes, *Industrial Relations, 1920-1930: a study of Dennison's "program for employee good will."* June 4, 1948, 100.

Round Robin cartoon, 1922.

outbreak of smallpox to some cities. Although the disease was not found in Framingham, Dennison offered vaccinations to its employees without charge. In the winter of 1929, cases of flu were rising. Fearful of a possible epidemic like that of 1918, a list of common-sense preventive rules was compiled and promoted in the January *Round Robin.* To prevent potential health hazards within the factory, the Company physician checked ventilation, lighting, heating and other conditions in the factory once a month.

The clinic offered new services and the most recent medical information. An eye clinic was added to the Dental and Medical clinics in 1924. Appointments could be made with an occultist, from the Massachusetts Eye and Ear Infirmary in Boston who visited the factory one morning a week. The charge for an examination was $3. Dennison also made arrangements with two local Opticians who provided glasses to employees at a discount.

Dr. Murray and other medical personnel wrote up-to-date articles for *Round Robin* that covered health care concerns. Titles included: *Can Cancer Be Conquered? First Aid At Home, Common Dangers of Colds,* and *How to Use Iodine.* Quite often, full page reminders stressed wholesome

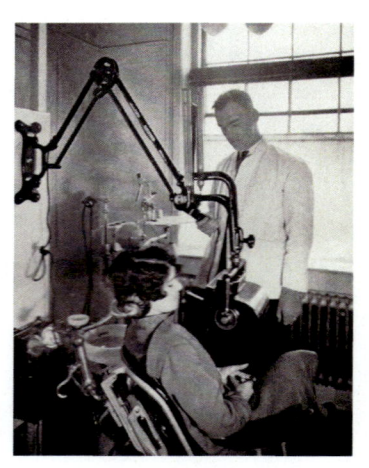

Dr. E.C. Stewart using the new x-ray machine. Miss Helen Casey of the clinic is 'the patient.' — *Round Robin,* February 1926.

practices: A diet of fruits and vegetables; meats and sweets in moderation and eight glasses of water each day, combined with exercise and proper rest was advised. These were among the essentials of good health promoted by Dennison. Does this sound familiar?

DENNISON ASSOCIATES – MEN / THE GIRLS' CLUB

A wide range of activities for men and women were available through Dennison's many clubs, sport teams, music and theatre groups.

Membership in these organizations offered social and educational opportunities. Each group was independent and had its own facility. Officers, managers and appointed committees for sports, entertainment, housing, education and publicity were elected annually to keep the clubs running smoothly.

Dennison Associates was first organized in 1911 by a group of men known as the "dinner club." Their first Club House was on Clinton Street. As membership increased, the group moved into a section of Building One.

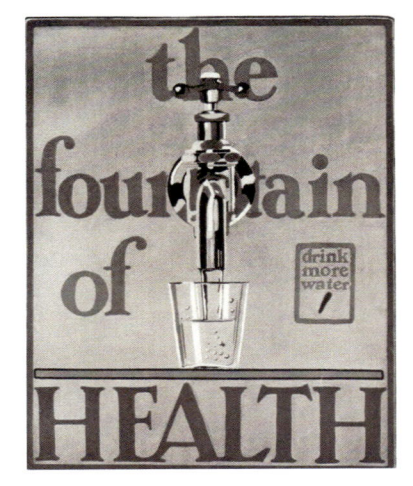

Round Robin full page reminders promoted good health.

Dennison Associates Club House, 1919.

ROVND ROBIN

CLVB
HOVSE
NVMBER
MAY 1928

Round Robin cover showing Dennison Associates new and old homes and its many activities.

Installation of the new ventilator system that carried off tobacco smoke.

Membership grew to 700 associates in the 1920s, which brought about the need for a much larger facility. After considerable planning, on April 27, 1928, a new Dennison Associates Club House opened in the former Building Six on Bishop Street. First-rate amenities were available in the remodeled two story building: a gym, four bowling alleys, six billiard tables, a library, and a card room. Of particular interest was a ventilation system that cleared the building's air six times an hour. Well, that made sense! The club had specifically advertised an abundance of ash trays on each floor. "Smokes" were very popular! Another draw to become a member was a 25% discount card at Kynoch's Sporting Goods Store, which was located right near the factory on Concord Street.

"Smokes," *Round Robin* cartoon, 1929.

The committees organized dances, sport teams, vaudeville, movies and outing of all sorts. One hundred members who watched the Bruins defeat the Rangers 2-1 at the Boston Garden on March 5, 1929, excitedly agreed it was a game of historical significance. Fred Bartolussi, Joe Clough, and a few others looked forward to sharpening their marksmanship on the new skeet shooting field at the Ox Bow Gun Club in Saxonville. And then there was the annual Ladies' Night. Music, Dance and Entertainment — not to be missed! Perhaps Charlie Woodward's original "Jazz Makers" would be on hand to play the latest tunes for this lively occasion.

Basketball Team, 1921.

Bowling League, 1924.

Round Robin cartoon, 1923.

Dennison Associates on the Charles River, 1916.

Skeet shooting at the Ox Bow Gun Club in Saxonville, 1929.

Charlie Woodward's "Jazz Makers," 1922.

Children begin to arrive at the Christmas Party, 1923.

Successful candy sales paid for
the Children's Christmas Tree Party.

Warner Bracken arrived at the party
in his sled, 1923.

Dennison Christmas Goods catalogue cover, 1918.

In 1925, 550 children attended the Christmas Tree Party.

*"The cost per child — 65 cents was more than met by the
Christmas Candy Sale."*– E.P. Hayes, *Industrial Relations*, 128.

For those with a sweet tooth, the Associates sponsored its annual Christmas Candy sale in November. The proceeds of the sale paid for the Children's Christmas Tree Party. In 1925, three tons of assorted candy was sold. Maybe *all* of Santa's expenses would be paid this year!

On a crisp December day, they arrived on foot, in carriages and in their parents' arms. Each year, several hundred party-goers were delighted by clowns, dancers, games, noisemakers and party hats. Music and merriment filled the air! Suddenly, shrieks of joy erupted at the sound of tinkling bells as Santa arrived with gifts for excited girls and boys. Maybe a youngster's longed for doll, bat or baseball mitt would be among the toys hidden away in Santa's sleigh. And at party's end, satisfied guests bustled out the door with pockets full of candy, the traditional Christmas orange in hand, and perhaps a sleepy grin appeared on each little reveler's face!

The Girls' Club house, located on the corner of Clinton and Grant Streets, opened on January 20, 1922. The attractive six room house included two sitting rooms, a kitchen, a sewing room, two rest rooms and a bath. Its porch was a popular place for fun, relaxation and dancing.

Card parties, showers, "organized sports"[6] and outings were among the many events arranged by the committees. A Saturday afternoon theatre party to see *Sally* at the Colonial Theatre was so enjoyable that the bewitched group stayed in Boston to attend a performance of *The Last Waltz* that very same evening. In response to the many invitations to "Ladies' Night" from the Men's Associates, the women hosted their first "Gentlemen's Night" at the Civic League Hall in 1923.

"Gentlemen's Night."
– *Parties: A Magazine of Decorations, Costumes – Games, Refreshments,* 1929.

Girls' Club house, 1922.

Along with the educational courses provided by the factory, informative and educational activities were also available through the Girls' Club. The winter of 1924 was especially busy. A variety of engaging evening classes was organized for the membership. Miss Elizabeth Abbot of the Advertising Department offered an arts and crafts class on Tuesday — *anything crepe* — party favors, flowers, lamp shades … and hats! Sewing instructor, Miss Rose Staunton of Framingham, taught dressmaking on Monday and Friday. It was a full week of classes when embroidery sessions were finally added on Wednesday evenings.

A graceful frock for winter events.
– *Round Robin,* "A Page of Interest to Women," December 1929.

Lamp shades, flowers and flower design ice cups were among the many crepe creations.

The girls enjoyed a bridal shower for Miss Louise Jones on the evening of June 29, 1922.

The women were attentive to the needs of the community. When the Framingham Hospital was in need of a new X-Ray machine, the group kindly donated ten dollars to the fund.

Members were encouraged to reserve the Club House for special occasions. On May 12, 1922, Miss Cecilia Goodwin celebrated her eighteenth birthday with friends at the Club House. Miss Lorna Kelley received many lovely packages at a bridal shower arranged just days before her marriage to Charles Sage of Framingham. Planned parties and surprise parties occurred quite frequently. The membership fee of 25 cents a month was surely a bargain!

In December of 1922, many of the ladies joined the Men's Associates in a performance of *The Rose Girl*, a musical comedy that was presented at Framingham's Gorman Theatre. The show promised "An All Star Cast, 100 Pretty Girls, Stunning Costumes and 1000 Laughs!"[7] Its promise was obviously fulfilled. The audience was utterly amused by this highly engaging production; so much so, that several shows soon

Get Your Tickets Now
for
The Rose Girl
given by
The Dennison Associates
at
The Gorman Theatre
on
MONDAY AND TUESDAY
EVENINGS
DECEMBER 18 and 19

An All Star Cast

100 Pretty Girls

Stunning Costumes

1000 Laughs

Cast of *The Rose Girl,* 1922.

followed. After an outstanding reception of the comedy/drama, *Buddies* in 1928, the Clubs planned to stage a joint show as an annual event.

Each group held an annual meeting, which began with supper, followed by a business update and ending with entertainment. In 1925, The Girls' Club ended their meeting with an amusing farce called *Ain't Women Wonderful!* Those in the audience clearly agreed: women are wonderful in their ability to change their minds!

The clubs within Dennison often organized functions together. They hosted a variety of mixed socials. Social interaction — "friendliness and unity within the factory"[8] was encouraged and enjoyed through the Company's many organizations.

Programs and activities were an integral part of the Dennison Manufacturing Company. The Company was always open to new ideas. As needs and interests arose, changes, additions and improvements were made in order to better serve the employees. The *Quarter Century Club* is an example of an organization that developed at the request of employees. In 1927, over 100 people who had worked at Dennison for twenty-five years or more wished to form a social club. Frank Doughty of the Box Department, first presented the club's plan to the Works Committee, and then to management, where it was enthusiastically accepted. In April, the *Quarter Century*

The Gorman Theatre.

124 members of the Dennison Quarter Century Club enjoyed their first annual banquet held at the Wellesley Inn on Saturday evening, June 11, 1927.

Club became a reality. On June 11, 124 members celebrated the Club's first banquet at the Wellesley Inn. At this time there were 176 members. The group represented more than 5,000 working years at Dennison!

In 1921, Henry Dennison gave a talk in which he stated, "In tackling any complex problems, it is extremely wise for us to recognize that betterment is a process — that betterment cannot simply be installed. We should recognize that it has got to start out slowly, that it has got to grow."[9] The Company strove for improvement and innovation. Its ability to join forces, to recognize the voices of management and factory brought success, and the development of many outstanding labor and social practices. *Some Dennison Plans and Practices* suggests: "Students of industrial progress may find a significance in the percentage figures on labor turnover for the Company over five-year periods:"

1913 .... 55%	
1918 .... 65%	***An impressive and clear indication***
1923 .... 22%	***of employee satisfaction!***
1928 .... 18.2[10]	

Mr. Donald Prince,[11] voices this "satisfaction" in an interview conducted for the 1995 Dennison Oral History Project. Mr. Prince begins by saying,

Donald Prince, circa 1952.
Courtesy of Nancy Prince.

"I went to work for Dennison July 10, 1933 and I retired May 31, 1975 … I started working for Dennison then, and I never regretted it … One thing I think Dennison tried to do was to give their customers quality merchandise at a fair and reasonable price. I think they also tried to be fair with employees whether they were in clerical positions, management positions or operating machines. Dennison tried to pay a fair and competitive wage, give fringe benefits … Dennison was a good place to work …"

Group of employees in front of office.
Courtesy of Susan Silva.

Women's Field Day Baseball Team, Norumbega Park, 1924.

Kindergarten class in the Lunch Room Vegetable Garden, 1918.

Henry S. Dennison: *A Tribute*

For more than fifty years, Henry S. Dennison was a prominent figure at the Dennison Manufacturing Company. Countless business and personal records point to a man of unmatched dedication and love for the Company, its employees and the town of Framingham. Under his dynamic leadership, the Dennison Manufacturing Company became one of the most successful and respected paper products companies in the world.

Mr. Dennison's business expertise led to memberships and appointments on local, state and Federal committees, conferences and commissions.

Henry S. Dennison at his desk.
Courtesy of the Library of Congress.

Mr. Dennison (left) often visited the departments. Machine shown is a two color-two sided shipping tag printer. September 20, 1920.

His numerous affiliations included:

Memberships

Boston Chamber of Commerce

The Taylor Society

Framingham Board of Trade / Chamber of Commerce

Framingham Emergency Reconstruction Committee, 1932

Appointments

Massachusetts Governor David Walsh's Pension Committee, 1915

President Wilson's Industrial Conference, 1919

Director of the Service Relations Division of the United States Post Office, 1922-1928

President Warren Harding's Unemployment Conference and the Coal Commission, 1922

Chairman of Fundraising – New building project-Framingham Union Hospital, 1926

President Franklin D. Roosevelt's Business Advisory Council of the U.S. Department of Commerce, 1933

Committee to oversee the Framingham TB Study sponsored by the Metropolitan Life Insurance Company, 1916-1923

First American Employers' Representative to the International Labor Office of the League of Nations, 1935-1939

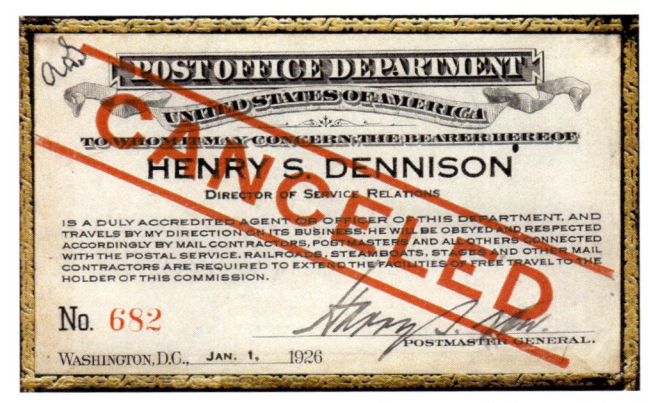

Director of Service Relations – United States Post Office, 1926.

WORLD WAR II CONTRIBUTION

Mr. Dennison could be seen atop Nobscot Mountain flying big box kites. While many thought it just a hobby, his main purpose was to test wind drift and air currents. Shortly after these investigations, thousands of small paper parachutes with dangling metallic foil strips, rained down from American bombers, jamming German radar. When the Government sought out a company to make these chutes, Mr. Dennison knew exactly what was needed.

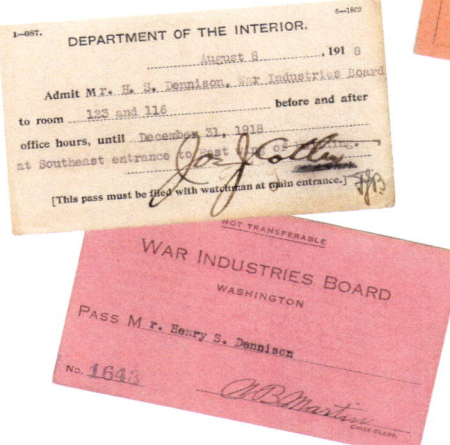

Government board pass cards: United States Shipping Board, War Trade Board, Department of the Interior, War Industries Board.

GIFTED SPEAKER AND PROLIFIC WRITER

Mr. Dennison was a dynamic speaker and an influential writer. In the 1920s and 1930s, among his varied speaking engagements, he addressed students at universities and colleges throughout the United States. A favorite theme for these speeches and lectures was "business management, a profession."[1] A particularly acclaimed speech, *Business and Government,* was given at the Honors Convocation at the University of Michigan in 1935.[2]

Mr. Dennison expressed his views in pamphlets, articles, books and reports. One of his books, *Organization Engineering* published in 1931, stressed the importance of reorganizing business according to the ever-changing business environment. In 1938 he wrote *Modern Competition and Business Policy* with J.K. Galbraith. And in the same year, Mr. Dennison authored *Toward Full Employment* with Lincoln Filene, Ralph E. Flanders, and Morris E. Leeds.[3]

FINAL TESTIMONIALS

In the late 1930s and 1940s, due to ill health, Mr. Dennison placed the active direction of the Company into the hands of his Vice-President, John S. Keir. As president, he continued to work in an advisory capacity and served as chairman of the Director's meetings. On February 29, 1952, after thirty-five years as Dennison's President, this accomplished business icon of the 20th century passed away. J.K. Galbraith in his 1981 Memoirs stated, "In 1937, Henry Dennison, then fifty-nine, was arguably, the most interesting businessman in the United States."[4]

Of equal importance to his innumerable business achievements, was the human aspect of his being. In an essay entitled *H.S.D. – As His Family Knew Him,* Edmund Ware Smith, eloquent writer and son-in-law of Henry S. Dennison captures his essence with these touching words:

"The four passionate devotions of this man's life were home and family on Juniper Hill, the 'shop', Dobsis[5] and humanity. Since H.S.D. frequently explored all four in a single burst of speech, you felt them inseparable in his heart and soul. They embraced and absorbed each other within him, the wellsprings of his being. His wisdom, wit and learning touched us all … He drank life in and poured it forth."[6]

Henry spent forty seasons at his beloved Camp Dobsis in Maine.

Upon Mr. Dennison's death, the March 12, 1952 Annual Town Meeting honored him with this memorial:

> RESOLVED, that in the death of Henry S. Dennison the Town of
>
> Framingham has suffered a major loss. He has rendered community services of
>
> a high order such as various citizens have performed through the years. But few
>
> citizens of this community have filled so large a place in the practical welfare
>
> of our people — few indeed have made their names so widely representative
>
> of principles in industrial management as Henry S. Dennison has done in
>
> Framingham during this first half of the Twentieth Century.[7]

In one of his annual reports, Mr. Dennison said this about the end of life:

"In this life I can never be certain of the real results of my efforts for good or ill ...The absolute measure of men is the extent to which they have operated to capacity — be that capacity what it may — in the service of their fellows."[8]

As the archives continue to reveal the life of Henry S. Dennison, it is *clear* that it would take a substantial volume to fully acknowledge his many far-reaching and valued accomplishments.

HENRY STURGIS DENNISON

March 4, 1877 - February 29, 1952

Entered the Employ of the
Company July 17, 1899

Director 1909 • Treasurer 1912 • President 1917

Dennison parade float in Framingham, circa 1922.

Epilogue

Dennison and Framingham became *One*. The Company was the town's largest employer as well as a magnanimous benefactor. An article featured in the booklet, *Town of Framingham Souvenir, 1906*, stresses and summarizes the unique relationship of this remarkable industry and the town of Framingham. The article describes Dennison as:

> ... *Framingham's chief source of prosperity and having an unrivalled plant and unsurpassed facilities that places it foremost in the manufacture of it special lines of production ... Some 1600 skilled hands are employed ... it has made the name of Framingham familiar to the world ... and has been an important factor in the upbuilding of the town. Even more, it has given an impetus to business, the home life, the school and the church, not only here but in surrounding towns.*

Delving into the archives highlighted the significance of Dennison's relationship to Framingham. Further probing led to *Welcome to Dennison Manufacturing Co.* This publication is the story of the foundation upon which Dennison was built. It describes the organization's formative history and its products, programs, and people. These were the essential building blocks of Dennison's future. The content is derived from the vast store of reports, photographs, studies and correspondence "unearthed" from the Dennison legacy.

Welcome to Dennison Manufacturing Co. is heuristic; its goal is to stimulate the interest of others and encourage additional investigation into the Dennison story utilizing this fascinating historical collection. As the archives continue to unfold, what is both expected and unexpected has been uncovered. Dennison has revealed itself as a multi-faceted gem through a broad range of historical accounts and artifacts found in its treasury. These materials provide a rich source for writers who wish to continue the Dennison narrative with their own themes and objectives in mind. The range of possibilities could fill volumes!

TIMELESS TREASURES

The history of the Dennison Manufacturing Company is told through its Archives. Nestled within the boxes, files and folders of the collection are many unexpected treasures. These documents, images and products not only tell the story of a prominent manufacturing company, but they reflect the societal trends, mores and events of the times. Timeless Treasures is a lasting Keepsake of the past — Enduring Memories of "The Way We Were."

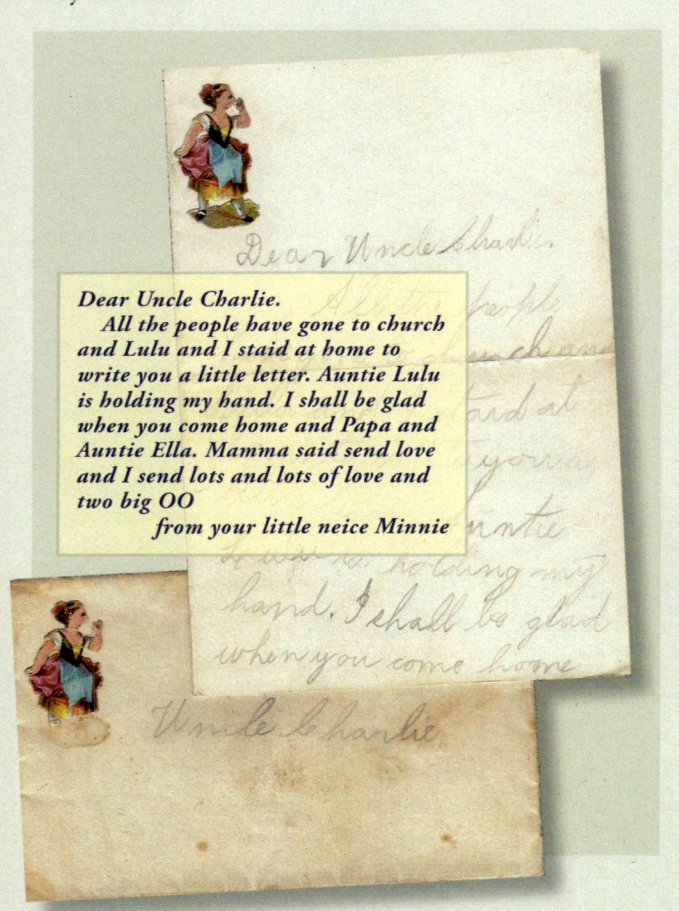

Dear Uncle Charlie.
All the people have gone to church and Lulu and I staid at home to write you a little letter. Auntie Lulu is holding my hand. I shall be glad when you come home and Papa and Auntie Ella. Mamma said send love and I send lots and lots of love and two big OO
from your little neice Minnie

Cover designed by illustrious artist Katherine Sturges Dodge, 1922.

A Purrfect Smile! 1929.

Letter to Charles Dennison from Minnie Dennison, Circa 1876.

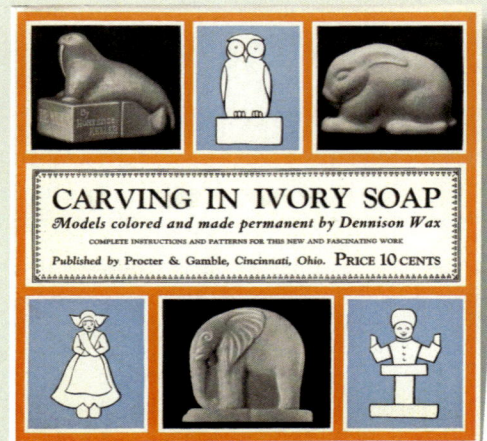

Carving in Ivory Soap, 1927.

Lesson – How to Carve a Duck, 1927.

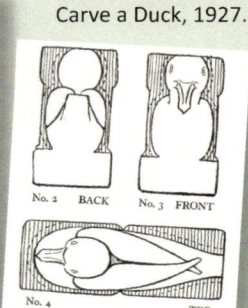

98

Dennison catalogue advertising Mickey Mouse products, 1931.

Dennison often promoted products by attaching samples in early catalogues. Dennison Stars, circa 1961, were purchased at *Building #19,* Natick, MA in 2013.
Courtesy Patricia Lavin.

Dennison factory "Outing" announcement, 1924.

99

One of many beautifully designed letterheads, 1910.

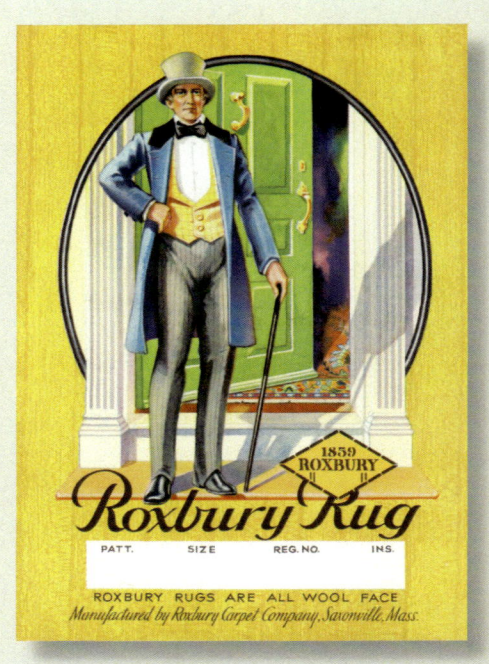

Label – Roxbury Carpet Company, Saxonville, Massachusetts.

Dennison Baseball Team, 1911.

The art of advertising, 1923.

Dennison Swim Team, 1921.

A proposal for a new Dennison building sign, 1904.

Cover – pictorial publication created for Dennison employees in the service, WW II, 1943.

Thank you to Dennison for a special Christmas package, signed Corporal James Graham, Jr., WW I, 1917, France.

Dennison Box Salesman, Steve Higgins, (first on left) among the group in Los Angeles at the end of the first scheduled Transcontinental Trip by Train and Plane. (Amelia Earhart holds flowers, Charles Lindberg third from right.) 1929.

Postcard – Transcontinental Air Transport flight sent to Dennison from passenger Steve Higgins. (Colonel Lindberg piloted flight from Clovis, New Mexico to Los Angeles.) 1929.

Holiday gift catalogue, 1902.

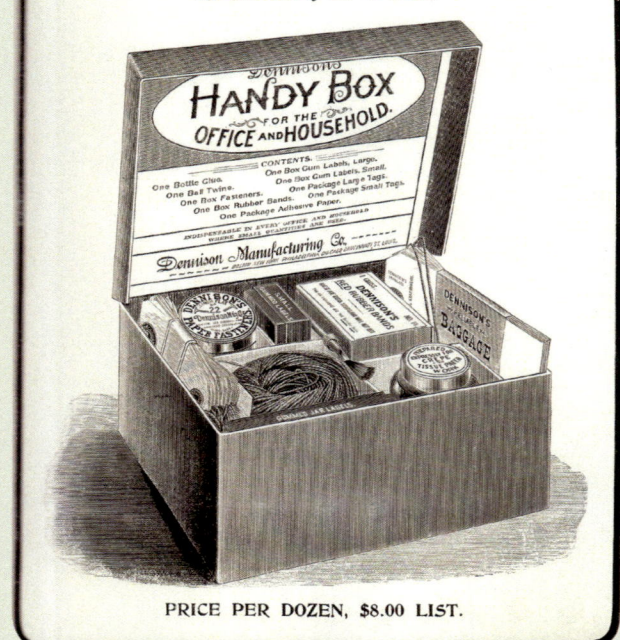

DENNISON'S HANDY BOX
FOR THE OFFICE AND HOUSEHOLD.

Contains Baggage Tags, Gummed Labels, Glue, Twine, Paper Fasteners, Rubber Bands, Key Tags and Adhesive Paper.

A quick selling article, appealing at once to all who see it, as handy to have in the house and office.

Retails readily for 75 cents.

PRICE PER DOZEN, $8.00 LIST.

Handy Box, "The Careful Housekeeper," 1896.

Extravagant crepe paper costume, 1911.

The reinforced patch, February, 1908.

Crepe paper designed to celebrate the opening of King Tut's tomb, 1923.

What Next? publication for shopkeepers, 1924.

102

NEW ACQUISITIONS
Courtesy of Rosemary Noble, Ellicott City, MD, 2015.

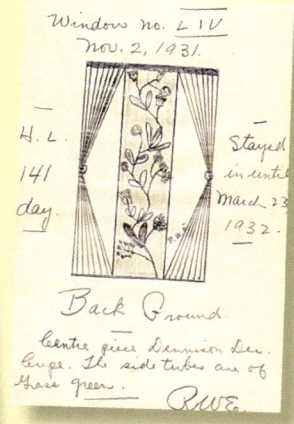

Tag Waltz – Composed by Bessie W. Fitzhugh for Dennison's fiftieth anniversary, 1894.

Forty-eight page booklet, *"How To Put The Win In Windows"* – illustrations and instructions for window displays, 1929. (owned by Russell W. Elliott).

Window Collection – example of a window background drawn by Russell W. Elliott, 1931. Mr. Elliott, a self-taught window decorator, kept a store and installed windows for shops in his home town of Cambridge, MD. His window sketches were inspired by a variety of Dennison window display publications.

The original *Round Robin!* 1916.

Crepe paper innovation – decorated harmonica box, 1920s.

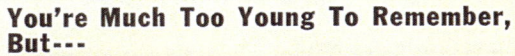

Dennison horse and buggy service to/from the South Framingham railroad station, early 1900s.

103

What influences the first sales of Powders and Perfumes?

THE *eye,* before the sense of smell, picks out the daintiest box or package. The powder in the tempting box is sure of a first trial, just as the powder which *pleases* is sure of a second trial. In quality, then, your box must equal your product.

The boxes which Dennison manufactures are as inviting as the products they enclose — and as distinctive. One look at the varieties of interesting samples on this page will convince of the beauty and taste conceived in manufacturing them.

And Dennison boxes are quality boxes because for seventy-five years Dennison skilled workers have made boxes for Perfumers, Jewelers and other exacting trades. Write for samples and prices.

Dennison Manufacturing Co.

MAKERS OF FINE BOXES
Works at Framingham, Mass.

Boston, 26 Franklin St.   New York, Fifth Ave. and 26th St.
Philadelphia, 1007 Chestnut St.   Chicago, 62 East Randolph St.
Sales Offices in 24 cities in the United States and Canada

London   Copenhagen   Mexico City   Buenos Aires   Rio de Janiero

Notes

The Dennison Story: *Product Evolution*

1. Andrew Dennison supported his large family by making and repairing shoes. As business competition began to increase, and ready-made shoes became available, he found his earnings and profit began to dwindle. Aaron hoped that the creation of a well-made box would not only benefit jewelers, but offer his father a more profitable and prosperous business.

2. With $20,000 backing from Mr. Curtis, the Roxbury watch factory was completed in 1851 — the first of its type in the world. In return for his investment, four hundred pocket watches manufactured at the Roxbury factory were inscribed with the name "Samuel Curtis."

3. As the line of merchandise steadily increased, E.W. moved to 163 Milk Street in 1858 where he hung his sign: "E.W. Dennison – Tag Manufacturer." Like 203 Washington Street, this site housed a small salesroom and factory for cards and tags. In 1885, Dennison moved to 26 Franklin Street, Boston.

4. It is possible that the New York location opened in 1853. A billhead dated January 1, 1854 was found with the 17 Maiden Lane address. Business in New York continued to grow. Over the years, Dennison moved to increasingly larger facilities. By 1912, the Company was located at prestigious 220 Fifth Avenue.

5. E.W. was called the "leader and builder" in several Dennison publications.
The Dennison Manufacturing Company (Framingham, Massachusetts, 1922), 4.

6. E.W. opened a box shop on the second floor of the Poland Block when the old Homestead could no longer accommodate the increase in business. In 1863, Matilda Dennison Swift set up a box shop under her own name. The site was located on the third floor of the Day Block (Swift Block) at the corner of Maine Street and Mason. Matilda manufactured J.I. Troche boxes for her brother, E.W., "on a salary and commission basis."
Charlotte Heath, *Dennison Beginnings: 1844-1878* (Dennison Manufacturing Company, 1927), 63.

Dennison Manufacturing Company, "Guide to Brunswick for Dennison Visitors," October 8, 1928.

7. Three years before incorporation E.W. wrote, "I am working quite hard to get our business into a form to pass to the good helpers we have as an inheritance. I am planning to incorporate it. Our helpers will become stockholders, their stock to be paid for in the profits of the company." The grandson of E.W., Henry S. Dennison, who became the Company's president in 1917, was highly influenced by this idea.
The Dennison Manufacturing Company, 1922, 10.

8. As Dennison added products, they were classified into groups or "lines" that suited different types of purposes – the Jewelers' Line, Dealers' Line, Stationers' Line, Crepe Line, Holiday Line etc. As the times changed, products were added and subtracted from the various lines based on sales. A clever box was added to the jewelry line in 1924. To draw attention to birthstone jewelry, boxes were covered with the color that matched the birthstone for each month.

9. Dennison Manufacturing Company, *Fifty Years: 1844-1894* (New York: Charles F. Bloom, 1894), 21.

10. At this time profits were extremely limited and E.W. was in need of business capital. Albert Metcalf had proven influential in business and was a natural at handling finances. This led E.W. to address Albert with these words: "Metcalf, how much can you raise?" Albert answered, "Well, I guess about $5,000." On these words, E.W, told Albert he wanted him to come into the business and offered to change the original name of the Company. Albert saw no need to change the name. The first papers for the firm Dennison & Company were drawn up by Albert's own hand on May 1, 1863. Along with Albert Metcalf, Henry Hawks (New York office) and William Spear (Foreman of the Newtonville box plant) became part of the newly formed co-partnership for a term of three years.
Heath, *Dennison Beginnings*, 59.

11. *Fifty Years: 1844-1894*, 22.

[12] The 1893 Chicago World's Fair (World's Columbian Exposition) was organized to celebrate the 400th Anniversary of Christopher Columbus's arrival in the New World. It was meant to highlight the World's progress over the past 400 years.
Dennison found fairs, conventions and expositions a valuable way to introduce goods to thousands of people at one time. Booth displays were tailored to fit the interest of the attendees. A teacher's convention might focus on crepe paper and other products for classroom project work. Events for the general public would generally concentrate on arts and crafts materials. Appropriate demonstrations and instructions were always available for each event.

[13] Exerpts from a letter written by J.A. Boyce in the 1929 March-April *Round Robin,* referred to the stringing of tags done in Falmouth, Massachusetts. About 1860, E.W.'s sister, Matilda Swift, placed this task in the hands of local families. The work was supervised by Annie R. Boyce, the letter writer's mother. Tags were sent from the factory to the Monument Railroad Station and were brought twelve miles by stagecoach to Falmouth. As business increased, the stringing of tags was moved to a small building on Mrs. Boyce's property. About 1872, a two story building was added. In the same year, the Woods Hole Branch of the railroad was finished, which then brought the tags right into West Falmouth. Several years later the building was moved to a site near the station where it was known as the Tag Shop. "With still increasing business, sub-agencies were started in various parts of Falmouth, Nantucket, Martha's Vineyard, West Brewster ..."

[14] "A wave of wartime expansion had caught all northern industry on its crest and was carrying it along almost in spite of itself."
Heath, *Dennison Beginnings,* 62.

[15] In 1865, the gummed labels were advertised as "Stratton's Gummed Labels." A few years later Mr. Dennison purchased the label rights and they were sold as Dennison Gummed Labels.

[16] This booklet was written by a Boston newspaperman under the direction of Dennison's Preston Pond, manager of the Boston store.

[17] F.E. Ewing *Reminiscences,* July 7, 1914, 12-14.

[18] In 1894, Sawyer and F.C. Brown of the Brooklyn Factory figured out a way to manufacture crepe. "The crepe effect was produced by running wet tissue paper round the cylinder against which a fine-edged knife was attached. The process was perfected and the new product launched in 1895."
Charlotte Heath, *Summary of Dennison History, 1878-1897* (Dennison Manufacturing Company, 1929), 27.

[19] As Dennison was working on ways to increase crepe's popularity, a fortunate accident occurred: "A pile of crepe rolls which fell on to a color slab in the Brooklyn shop demonstrated the possibilities of tinted crepe." This was then followed by experiments with a second-hand wall-paper machine, which led to the development of printed or decorated crepe.
Heath, *Summary of Dennison History,* 30.

[20] The first costume show was held a few years earlier in the Chicago store. In the spring of 1923, the shows were held simultaneously in all four stores for the first time. "The purpose of the display is to reveal the possibilities of crepe paper for pageant, and party costumes." It was also a time to highlight a variety of crepe paper products for decorative purposes.
"The Big Event of the Year in Our Stores," *What Next? Dennison Bulletin,* March 1924, 6.

[21] On October 12, 1926, the first in a series of Craft Talks given by instructor Dorothy Wright was broadcast from stations in Boston, (WEEI) New York, (WEAF) Philadelphia, (WLIT) and Washington. (WRC) In addition to flower making, unique holiday ideas were added to the ten lesson course.
Oct. 12 – A Harvest Party
Dec. 7 – Dennison dolls that children can make
Dec. 14 – New ways to decorate Christmas boxes
Dennison offered a free instruction guide that was sent to listeners upon request.
"Dennison Craft Lessons on Air from Four Stations," *Framingham News,* October 7, 1926.

Dennison received a letter dated October 20, 1926 from Mrs. Frank Hilt, wife of the lighthouse keeper on Manicius Rock Life Station. The Hilt's island home was located 18 miles off the coast of Maine. Mrs. Hilt wrote: "Last Tuesday afternoon I listened for the first time to your talk which was music to my ears as possibly you might think, when I write." She continued, "I would like to learn to make the flowers and you bet

I shall listen in, next Tuesday if all is well and will you inform me what is needed for the flowers and where I can get the material?" At the end, she added: "We have a radio and get all the good things put on the air." Mrs. Hilt heard the program from WEEI in Boston. This letter showed how Dennison's experimental radio talks were available to those who might not be reached by other means.
"Eighteen Miles Out, Tunes in On Our Radio Talks," *Round Robin*, January 1927, 19.

22 "What Would You Do Without It – and what is more important – what are you doing with it?"
What Next? 1928, 4.

23 As products were developed, buyers often said to Dennison, "What Next?" This question led to the publication, *What Next?* Each *What Next?* issue meant for shopkeepers, was filled with how-to recommendations, the newest product idea and trends, along with clever marketing ideas to promote sales. Featured promotional hints included:
• *Sealing Wax Lore* – each wax color was meant to convey a different meaning: Ruby, engaged lovers, Pink, youthfulness and Blue, constancy. Remember these sentiments when you next seal a special letter!
• *A Lesson in Window Dressing* included twelve points for a successful window: Clean glass inside and out, use simplicity and common sense, group articles that go together … illuminate at night. Finally, add a descriptive card or a poster to get your message out. What a perfect way to catch the passing window gazer's eye!
• *New Developments in Sealing Wax Art* illustrated the latest in wax crafts. In 1924, painting of pottery with sealing wax was very popular. Dennison suggested shopkeepers display samples of pottery before and after wax painting, set out sealing wax sticks and a few sealing wax circulars to draw the interest of potential customers. Or perhaps an instructional class might be of interest to crafters. The many *What Next?* suggestions were offered in a gentle friendly way.

The Holiday Line: *A Novel Idea!*

1 The Holiday Line was first seen as a "devise by which production would be evened out throughout the year." By the 1920s and 1930s the volume of sales was high, but the profit was not. Sales from 1924-1929 amounted to three and a half million dollars, but profit only

totaled eighteen thousand dollars. The end of the next decade brought losses. Attracting new markets and changing the "mix" of merchandise led to outstanding profit in the 1940s. From 1946-1952, sales amounted to about thirty-three million dollars, 17% of the Company's total for this period. The history and the success of the Line at this time, led the Company to conclude: handled properly, "We will always hope and expect it will be good reading in solid black figures." D.C. Huntington, editor, *John S. Keir* (Portland, Maine: Anthoesen Press, 1960), 27-30.

Historian Charlotte Heath gives credit to Dennison President, Henry Dyer of New York and Preston Pond, manager of the Boston Store as originators of the Holiday Lines.
Charlotte Heath, *The Christmas Line: A Suggestive Study*, Dennison Manufacturing Company, December 1928, 10.

2 The first items used for gifts came from the box line. Boxes used for holidays dated back to 1850. "Picture top boxes for Christmas trade are mentioned in 1876. Game sets and jewelry cleaning caskets were introduced during the 'Seventies; jewel cabinets, wax sets, tissue paper outfits, and Wilson's gummed letters in a Handy Box during the 80's; and the Dennison Handy Box in the '90's."
Heath, *The Christmas Line*, 3-4.

3 An exciting example of matching event to product quickly followed the opening of Egyptian King, Tutankhamen's tomb, in February of 1923. The Tomb's discovery filled the newspapers with a stream of articles and pictures, which brought about "a vogue for Egyptian styles." An employee suggested that an Egyptian design should be added to the Decorated Crepe papers to commemorate the event. This idea was immediately accepted by the Crepe Committee. An artist was then asked to fashion a design, which was approved on March 10th. The new design with five colors "was running on a crepe printing machine in Department 21" on March 28th. In April, this new design was ready to be sold for the creation of the most "fashionable" Egyptian parties. Dennison called the production of this design, "Some Speed."
Dennison Manufacturing Company, *Round Robin "Our New 'King Tut' Crepe,"* April 1923, 7.

4,5 Heath, *The Christmas Line*, 4.

6 Handy boxes contained an assortment of stationery products packed in partitioned boxes. They were designed with appropriate items for use in schools, homes, offices and stores. Box content varied according to purpose. Among the items that might be included were: glue, paper fasteners, tags, twine, assorted labels, paper clips ....

7 Heath's study, *The Christmas Line, 6-7,* noted that the information about the holly seal came from *Recollections, 1922* – Mr. Pond of the Boston Store. (She also added this information about the seal: where it came from we do not know.)

8 Mr. James Armington was hired by Dennison as an errand boy in 1886. In 1890, he became a tag salesman for the Boston territory as the Holiday Lines were developing. He held several managerial positions over the years. As Dennison Crepe Paper Specialist in 1928, he promoted the sale of crepe products to the Company's large markets throughout the United States. After 44 years of service, Mr. Armington retired in 1929. Dennison Manufacturing Company, *Round Robin "News Bits from Everywhere,"* December 1929, 14.

9 Heath, *The Christmas Line,* 9.

10 Dennison hired artists to design products and also to illustrate its publications. Katherine Sturges Dodge and Lang Campbell were among the prominent illustrators.

Katherine Sturges Dodge illustrated several children's books for the P.F. Volland Company from 1913-1921. She also wrote and illustrated her own books. Among these were: *Peeps The Really Truly Sunshine Fairy* in 1918 and *Tales of Little Dogs* in 1921.

Lang Campbell was best known as the illustrator of the *Uncle Wiggly Series.* Campbell also created pictures of Br'er Rabbit. He wrote and illustrated his own book, *The Funny Feathers* in 1917. *Merry Murphy,* an Irish potato story presented as a rebus, was written and illustrated by Mr. Campbell in 1929. In the 1930s, he created his own cartoon strips – *Piggy Pigtail, Dippy Doodleburg* and others.

11 In the 1920s, sales showed it was clear that the public wanted familiar Christmas designs. Dennison concluded: "While we are very alive to the chance to introduce new symbols, our progress must be largely in new and better uses of old symbols." Heath, *The Christmas Line,* 38.

The Company found in the late 1950s that, "The finished line must contain a definite proportion of strong "basic" designs – motifs such as Santa, holly, bells, candles ... which Dennison has found the public likes best, must be created in a fresh new style." "A Christmas Custom," *Shell News,* December 1956, 12.

12 Hallowe'en was the contraction for "All Hallows Eve:" (October 31) a spelling that was often used during this time period. Heath, *The Christmas Line,* 9.

13 The *Bogie Book* was named after mischievous Halloween spirits. *Bogie Books* appeared annually after 1912 except for 1918. (The 1918 Influenza Epidemic may have been responsible for the omission this year. Gatherings were restricted.) Along with Halloween suggestions, the issues included entertaining ideas for Harvest, Thanksgiving and New Year celebrations.

In 1927, the *Bogie Book,* the *Christmas* Book and the *Gala Book* were discontinued. These were replaced with the new *Dennison Party Magazine,* which was published six times each year. It was filled with suggestions for decorations and entertainment for special holidays using Dennison products.

The following paragraph from the 1909 *Bogie Book* is an example of Dennison's Halloween marketing: "Any hostess can easily select from this little book the scheme of decoration, games and favors that will best entertain the guests she wishes to please. All the articles described are easily made, with Dennison crepe paper and a little effort. Anyone can accomplish the results desired. If any difficulty arises, the paper experts at the Dennison stores will be glad, by correspondence or personally, to explain and demonstrate." Michele Behan, "The Hair-Raising Prices of Dennison's Bogie Books." *Book Think – Resources for Booksellers.* October 29, 2007. http://www.bookthink.com/0106/106beh1.htm.

14 Dennison Manufacturing Company, *Round Robin "Gala Day,"* September 1925, 13.

The Next Step: *Transition*

1 Dennison Manufacturing Company, *E. W. Dennison: A Memorial* (Boston: B.D. Updike, The Merrymount Press, 1909), 79.

2 Henry B. Dennison, the older son of E.W. joined the Boston store in 1862. He successfully opened the Chicago branch in 1868 and returned to Boston the following year. He became Superintendent of factories

in1869. Upon the death of his father in 1886, Henry was elected president. Due to ongoing health issues Henry resigned in 1892. That same year, Henry Dyer of the New York store became Dennison's president. He began work as an errand boy in the New York store under Henry Hawks. Mr. Dyer worked his way up the ladder from clerk, to salesman … manager of the New York Store … to president in 1892. As a man who had worked from the bottom up, he was looked to for sales and merchandise leadership. Mr. Dyer retired in 1906 and was followed by the fourth president J.F. Talbot who resigned in 1909.

The Business Climate: *Nineteenth Century Framingham*

[1] The two men enjoyed a meal at the brick hotel and tavern owned by John Stone, a descendent of Framingham's first settler, John Stone. They then made speeches from the porch of the building's second floor. This same brick building is now the restaurant known as John Stone's Inn, which is located in the center of Ashland. The Ashland Post Office has a mural that commemorates this historic event.

[2] Stephen W. Herring, *Framingham: An American Town*, (Framingham: Framingham Historical Society, Framingham Tercentennial Commission, 2000), 142-143.

[3] Ibid, 196.

[4] Ibid, 185.

[5] H.M. Richardson employed forty people to make rocking horses in a vacant Prattville factory. (Pratt Street neighborhood) "The Harding brothers made canoes and built the first of many boat houses on Waushakum Pond."
Herring, 198, 211-212.

[6] Ibid, 212.

[7] At the time of the interview, John Collins was the Superintendent of Department 3, the gummed label cutting room. In 1883, Mr. Collins became an employee at Dennison's Milk Street location in Boston. He retired from Framingham after 44 years of service in December 1928. Upon his retirement, John was given a purse of gold along with good luck wishes from the members of his department. Everyone agreed, John's wonderful stories of Dennison's past would be missed.

[8] Herring, 212.

[9] Presidents who followed J.F. Talbot: Charles S. Dennison 1909-1912, Frank E. Ewing 1912-1917, Henry S. Dennison 1917-1952.

Centralization

[1,2] E.P. Hayes and Charlotte Heath, *History of the Dennison Manufacturing Company* (Cambridge, Massachusetts: Harvard University Press, 1929), 490, 496.

Policies and Practices

[1] Frederick Taylor's (1856-1915) scientific approach stressed the importance of cooperation between management and labor. This concept, along with Dennison's integration of marketing and manufacturing helped to promote the efficient flow of production. The principles of the Taylor movement led Henry "to approach business problems as a scientist and to stress profession rather than profit as a true goal for business management."
James T. Dennison, *Henry S. Dennison (1877-1952): New England Industrialist who Served America!* (New York: The Newcomen Society in North America, 1955), 14.

"Frederick Taylor and Scientific Management." *NetMBA.com*. 2010. http://www.netmba.com/mgmt/scientific/.

[2] Sample results of cooperation between the Works Committee and Management in 1920: (1) Promotions – Notices of positions would be posted on the Bulletin Boards so all employees would be aware of positions available to them. (2) Lunch Room – A special 35 cent lunch was introduced that included dessert and a beverage. (3) Co-operative Buying – A bulk buying program was developed for employees. (4) Car Shelters – As parking spaces became limited, management agreed to add three garages for employees' vehicles.

[3] The Plan provided an annual distribution of one-third of the profits available for distribution after dividends were paid. "The employees who receive this distribution must have been two years in the employ of the company at the beginning of the year in which the profits to be distributed were earned."
Dennison Manufacturing Company, *Dennison Institutions*, 1925, 11.

In 1925, 2,318 workers shared in Company earnings based on years of service. For example, those who had

worked at Dennison for more than two years, but less than five, received certificates valued at $60. Workers with twenty-five years of service and over received $150 in certificates.
Dennison Manufacturing Company, *Round Robin,* April 1925, 9.

In 1928, employees needed five years of service to share in the Plan.
Dennison Manufacturing Company, *Some Dennison Plans and Practices,* 1928, 11.

[4] Dennison Manufacturing Company, *The Annual Report to the Stockholders,* 1921, 16.

By 1925 Dennison employed more than 4,000 people. This included factory, stores and districts in the United States and abroad. "Over half of the employees are now Industrial Partners of the Company."
Dennison Manufacturing Company, *Book of Information,* 1925, 23.

[5] In 1921 the Fund contained $150,000. During this year $22,989.02 was distributed.
Some Dennison Plans and Practices, 16.

"People" Programs

[1] *Round Robin* had this to say about the value of the Dennison Library: "It's a wonder that Dennison people haven't become a swarm of bookworms with all the library service that is being offered to them these days. Not only can an employee take his pick of a large number of instructive and interesting volumes of the central library; he can sit down near his machine at noon now, and let the library come to him."

[2] Esther Staples, "A History Room That Pays Its Way," *Advertising and Selling* (August 1930).

[3] The Men's Glee Club performed within the factory and also held concerts for the public. In the 1920s, they traveled to Hopkinton, Wayland, Ashby, Springfield and surrounding towns to perform. Their annual concerts took place at the Lincoln School Hall, Framingham. In 1926, the proceeds from this event paid for a trip to Portland, Maine where the group took part in a competition sponsored by the New England Federation of Glee Clubs. Music lovers enjoyed a radio broadcast performed by the Glee Club, which was aired from the studio of Boston's WBZ in 1925. The success of this program led to a performance from Boston's Radio Station WEEI in December of the following

year. On February 22, 1928, the Club had the honor of performing at the dedication of Framingham's new town hall, the Memorial Building.

Dennison's first Girls' Glee Club concert was held on June 6, 1919 at the Grace Church in Framingham. It was a winner! The audience hoped that the concert would be one of many to come.

Dennison also had a mixed glee club.

[4] The first Women's Rest Room was a memorial dedicated to Mrs. Eliphalet Dennison in 1912. By 1916, a new room was added. About 60 patients were seen in the clinic each day. Mr. T.G. Portmore in a talk to the Managerial Industrial Partners in 1924 said the following about the Clinic: "… it gives everyone a greater sense of security … The chief aim of the Clinic is to reduce absent time through prevention of disease and by the immediate treatment of injuries. By keeping absent time at a minimum, the Clinic becomes a vital factor in production."

[5] The Life Extension Institute was made up of about 100 physicians, scientists, philanthropists and other forward-thinkers of the time. Former President William Howard Taft, Alexander Bell, Yale Economist Irving Fisher and Dr. Eugene Fisk were among its founding members. They influenced the medical field and businesses through their program, "The Growing Movement to Prolong Human Life." They stressed the annual physical examination and offered up-to-date health information. Prevention was the key!
"Field of Life Insurance," *The Standard,* January 3, 1914, 9-14.
"The Growing Movement to Prolong Human Life," *The Independent,* April 20, 1918, 135.

[6] Sports activities, including teams and tournaments were sponsored by the Factory and the clubs. Baseball, basketball, bowling, hiking, field days, tennis, and gym classes were among the activities that were available to both men and women. According to the September 1922 *Round Robin,* the annual outing to Norumbega Park, Auburndale, MA featured "Two Baseball Games and Sports of Every Description."

[7] *Round Robin,* December 1922, 3.

[8] *Dennison Institutions,* 1925, 21.

[9] *Dennison Institutions,* 2.

[10] *Some Dennison Plans and Practices,* 1928, 21.

[11] Donald Prince was a graduate of Harvard Business School in 1933. Mr. Prince held a variety of positions during his 42 year career at Dennison Manufacturing Company. Among these positions were General Manager of the Coated Paper Division, General Manager of Industrial Products and General Manager of Therimage. Therimage is a unique transfer process developed by Dennison in the 1950s. "Multi-colored labels are printed on release-coated paper and through the application of heat and pressure, the image is transferred to a plastic container." This process was eventually used on glass as well as plastic.
Donald Prince, Interview Transcription, *Dennison Oral History Project,* interviewed by Anita DeFelice, Sam Geschelin, 1995.
Kathy Coffey, *Case Study: Dennison Manufacturing Company,* 1982.

Henry S. Dennison: *A Tribute*

[1] H.S. Dennison diligently promoted business management as a profession. "In the course of lecture on business ethics at the University of California in 1932, he recurred to his favorite theme, business management, a profession: I believe that we can hope for progress in ethical standards and ethical behavior of the business world only in so far as we can hope that business management will advance toward the status which has already been reached by the rest of professional life …"
James T. Dennison, 22.

[2] The following paragraph gives some insight into H.S. Dennison's thoughts on Business and Government: "–until business can discover ways by which, and through which it can bring its motives for service to its employees and to the rest of the community up to the strength of its motives to serve its investors, business must expect an increasing government interference."
James T. Dennison, 24-25.

[3] In *Modern Competition and Business* Policy: "the authors combining economic theory and business experience suggested a number of measures that seemed necessary if modern capitalism is to have a fair chance to survive." In *Toward Full Employment*: "the authors as industrialist, who had felt the shock and accepted the challenge of depression, sought to diagnose the trouble and suggest remedies; for they believed that socially harmful unemployment should not exist in America…"
James T. Dennison, 26.

[4] John K. Galbraith, *A Life in Our Times* (Boston, Massachusetts: Houghton Mifflin Company, 1981), 61.

[5] Dobsis was H.S. Dennison's camp in the Maine Woods. Edmund Ware Smith, "H.S.D. – AS HIS FAMILY KNEW HIM," in *Henry S. Dennison* (c. 1952), 9.

[6] Edmund Ware Smith, 9-13.

[7] Town of Framingham. Published Town Report, "Resolution," 1952.

[8] "H.S.D. SPEAKS," in *Henry S. Dennison* (c. 1952), 7.

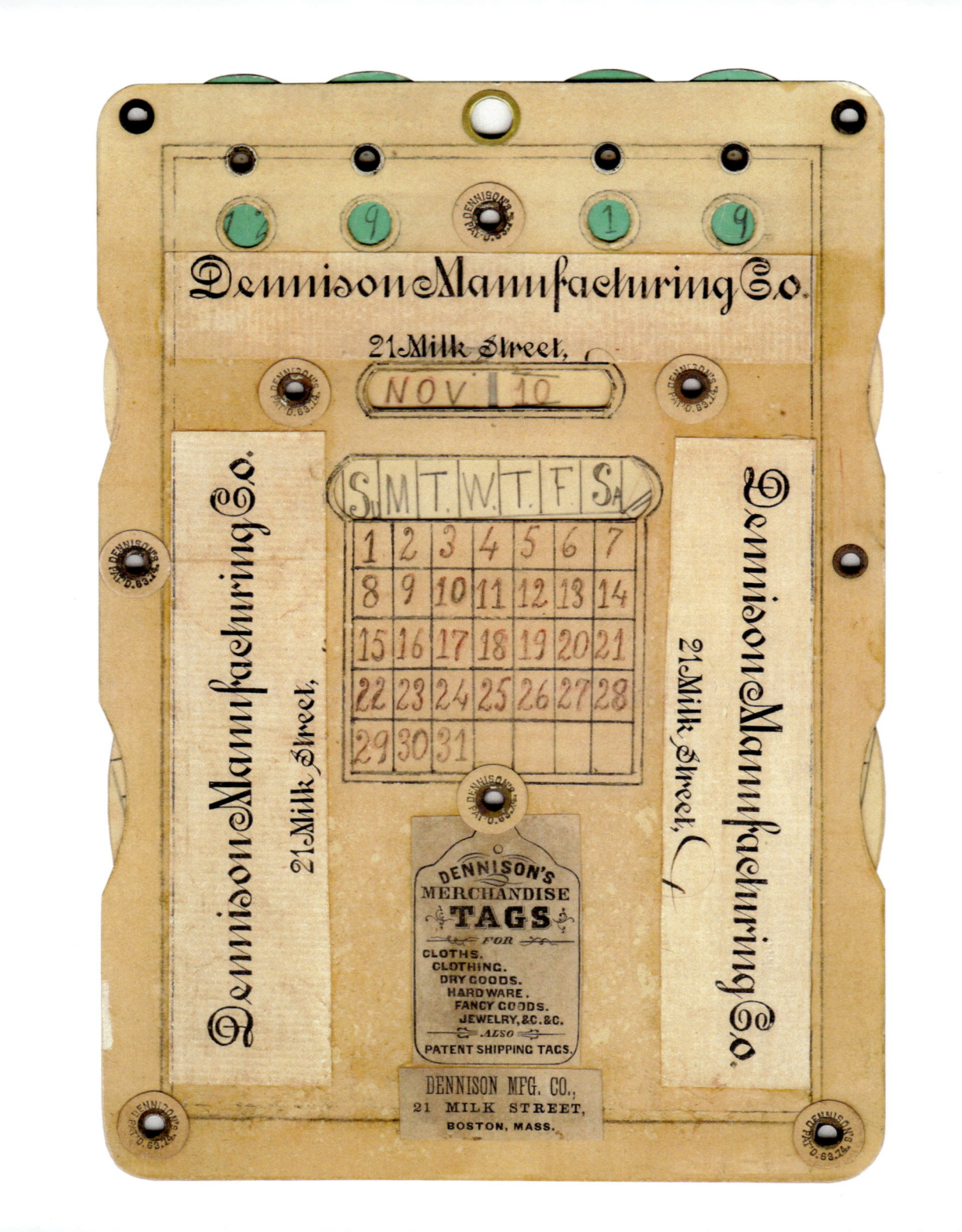

Bibliography

Articles

"A Christmas Custom." *Shell News,* December 1956.

Behan, Michele. "The Hair-Raising Prices of Dennison's Bogie Books." *Book Think – Resources for Booksellers.* October 29, 2007. http://www.bookthink.com/0106/106beh1.htm.

"Dennison Craft Lessons on Air from Four Stations," *Framingham News,* October 7, 1926.

"The Growing Movement to Prolong Human Life," *The Independent,* April 20, 1918.

"Frederick Taylor and Scientific Management." *NetMBA.com.* 2010. http://www.netmba.com/mgmt/scientific/.

Staples, Esther. "A History Room That Pays Its Way." *Advertising and Selling,* August 1930.

Books

Dennison Manufacturing Company. *E.W. Dennison A Memorial.* Boston, Massachusetts: Merrymount Press, 1909.

———. *Round Robin.* Volumes 1-23, 1909-1929.

———. *Seventy-Five Years: 1844-1919.* Framingham, Massachusetts, 1919.

———. *What Next? Dennison Bulletin,* 1924 and 1928.

Galbraith, John K. *A Life in Our Times.* Boston, Massachusetts: Houghton Mifflin Company, 1981.

Hayes, E.P., and Charlotte Heath. *History of the Dennison Manufacturing Company.* Cambridge, Massachusetts: Harvard University Press, 1929.

Heath, Charlotte. *Dennison Beginnings: 1840-1878.* Brunswick, Maine, 1927.

Herring, Stephen W. *Framingham: An American Town.* Framingham, Massachusetts: Framingham Historical Society, Framingham Tercentennial Commission, 2000.

Huntington, D.C., editor, *John S. Keir.* Portland, Maine: Anthoesen Press, 1960.

Booklets

Dauterman-Ricciardi, Dr. Dana. *Tag Town: Dennison's Legacy.* Framingham, Massachusetts: Framingham Historical Society and Museum, 2002.

Dennison, James T. *Henry S. Dennison (1877-1952): New England Industrialist Who Served America!* New York: The Newcomen Society in North America, 1955.

Dennison Manufacturing Company. *Book of Information,* 1925.

———. *Dennison Institutions,* 1925.

———. *Employee Guide for Framingham Complex,* 1988.

———. *Fifty Years 1844-1894,* 1894.

———. *Henry S. Dennison,* Recollections.

———. *Some Dennison Plans and Practices,* 1928.

———. *The Dennison Manufacturing Company,* 1922.

———. "One Hundred Years After Birmingham," 1912.

Framingham Board of Trade South Framingham, 1908-09.

"H.S.D. SPEAKS." In *Henry S. Dennison,* c. 1952.

Smith, Edmund Ware. "H.S.D. – AS HIS FAMILY KNEW HIM." In *Henry S. Dennison,* c. 1952.

Town of Framingham Massachusetts. *Souvenir,* 1906. Framingham, Massachusetts: Lakeview Press, 1906.

Collections

Framingham History Center Archives and Collections

Framingham Public Library – Dennison Collection – Framingham Room

Studies

Heath, Charlotte. *Home Work as A Factor In Dennison Production,* Dennison Manufacturing Company, 1928.

———. *Summary of Dennison History* 1878-1897, Dennison Manufacturing Company, c. 1920.

Heath, Charlotte. *The Christmas Line: A Suggestive Study,* Dennison Manufacturing Company, December, 1928.

Hayes, E.P. *Industrial Relations, 1920-1930: A study of Dennison's "program for employee good will."* June 4, 1948.

Case Studies

Cawein, Paul E. *The Dennison Manufacturing Company.* Case Studies in Business History and Economic Concepts. Vol.2. D.C. Heath & Co., 1967.

Coffey, Kathy. *Dennison Manufacturing Company,* May 11, 1982.

Gras, N.S.B., Larson, Henrietta. *Dennison Manufacturing Company 1844-1938,* Casebook in American Business History, Appleton-Century-Crofts, NY, 1939.

Vollmers, G. *An Introduction to the Company, Its Most Influential President and Its Archives.* The Accounting Notebook, April 1998.

Reports

Dennison Manufacturing Company. Report to Stockholders, 1920.

———. Report to Stockholders, 1921.

Town of Framingham. Published Town Report, 1952.

Interviews

Ewing, F.E. *Reminiscences,* July 7, 1914, 12-14.

Prince, Donald. Interview Transcription, *Dennison Oral History Project,* interviewed by Anita DeFelice, Sam Geschelin, 1995.

Index

Note: Pages with illustrations are in italics; *fn* denotes footnote number.

From the Authors

PATRICIA LAVIN

The Framingham History Center is dedicated to the preservation of Framingham's history. As a retired teacher and diehard history buff, I was naturally drawn to this spirited organization. The Center hosts public programs, exhibitions and tours. It offers volunteers an opportunity to participate in sharing this history with the community.

For me, one of these opportunities involved the transcription of Civil War letters in 2010. These interesting eyewitness accounts led to the publication of *My Dear Esty: Letters from Framingham's Civil War Soldiers* in 2011.

I was fortunate in the summer of 2012 to have been among those who first encountered the Dennison Archives at the Bishop Street Warehouse. As we combed through and organized the contents for transportation to its new home at the Framingham History Center, riveting stories presented themselves.

The images and documents highlighted the everyday life of Dennison's employees. Products, places, events and familiar family names gradually emerged. Within the collection, I found pictures and information about my grandmother, mother and other family members. Fascinating findings seemed endless.

Dennison Manufacturing Company's history, its contribution to Framingham and its people is an enduring legacy to be forever cherished.

LAURA STAGLIOLA

When author Pat Lavin came to me and asked if I would assist her with this book, it was an unexpected but very pleasant surprise. She explained that in order to clearly convey the Dennison story she needed someone to help her put together images of objects from the archives. Having worked with the Dennison archives previously, I immediately agreed.

I first came in contact with the Dennison Manufacturing Company in 2013 as the Tom Desilets Memorial Intern for the Framingham History Center. This internship was created to organize and sort through the Dennison archives which had recently returned to Framingham from California. Over the course of the internship, I became familiar with the rich collection of letters, product samples, corporate documents, photographs, and more. I was eager to work with Pat on this project because it is rare to find companies like Dennison nowadays.

As an enthusiastic young historian, I see immense value in preserving the history of companies like Dennison. This company took great pride in treating its employees like family, while also focusing on achieving product excellence and creating unique ways to advertise its goods; this is something I wish I could have the chance to experience as a customer in my lifetime. Pat's words and research have provided me with the opportunity to view the full scope of the Dennison Manufacturing Co. as a pioneer of American industry, and for that, I sincerely thank her.